A Year in Provence

Peter Mayle spent fifteen years in the advertising business, first as a copywriter and then as a reluctant executive, before escaping Madison Avenue in 1975 to write books. His work has been translated into seventeen languages, and he has contributed to the *Sunday Times*, the *Financial Times*, *The Independent*, *Gentlemen's Quarterly* and *Esquire*. He lives in Provence with his wife, three dogs, several builders and numerous guests. He is approaching fifty as slowly as possible.

A YEAR IN PROVENCE

PETER MAYLE

ILLUSTRATED BY
LESLIE FORBES

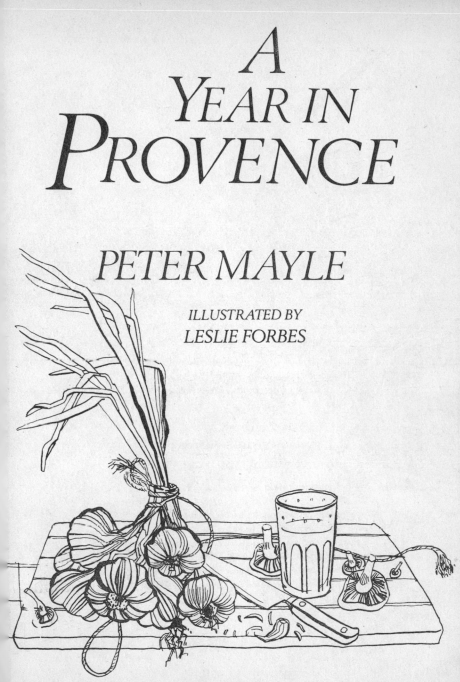

PAN BOOKS
London, Sydney and Auckland

First published in Great Britain in 1989 by
Hamish Hamilton Ltd, London

This edition published in 1990 by Pan Books Ltd,
Cavaye Place, London SW10 9PG

37 39 38 36

© Peter Mayle 1989
Illustrations © Leslie Forbes 1989

ISBN 0 330 31236 7

Printed in England by Clays Ltd, St Ives plc

To Jennie,
with love and thanks

PREFACE TO THE PAPERBACK EDITION

One sad change has taken place since this book was written. Monsieur Soliva, the husband of Tante Yvonne at Lambesc, has died and the restaurant has closed. He was a delightful old man, and we shall miss him.

Otherwise, life in Provence continues much as I have described it – slow, hot and pleasant in the summer; slow, cold and pleasant in the winter. We have lived here for three years now without a day's regret.

I have mixed feelings about the effects that the book has had on our lives. It is always wonderful to receive letters from readers, and the letters have come by the dozen, from places as varied as Beijing and Her Majesty's Prison at Wormwood Scrubs. It is sometimes less wonderful to find the reader on the doorstep, book in hand and tongue hanging out for a glass or two – flattering, but often so unexpected that I have more than once been caught literally with my trousers down. Signing books, dripping from the shower and dressed in a towel, has been a novel experience.

The only cloud on our horizon at the moment is a small one, no bigger than an estate agent's commission. There are hideous rumours of what our local friends call *un boum*. By 1992, they say, Provence will be firmly established as the California of Europe.

I hope they're wrong. It conjures up visions of diet-crazed water drinkers in double-knit pastel jogging ensembles, of cordless telephones by the pool and authentic Provençal-style jacuzzis next to the tennis court. I have a terrible feeling that the French would love it all. It's the refugees who hope that Provence will stay the way they found it.

But at least for today I can look out of the window and see nothing but vines and mountains, and hear no sound except my neighbour cursing his dead tractor. He'll stop at noon and go home for lunch, and then send his wife out to repair the tractor while he goes into the forest with his dog. The summer drought and the forest fires have driven most of the game far away, up towards the Basses Alpes, but hunters are optimists. And if no obliging rabbit or bird should present itself to the gun, *tant pis*. There's always tomorrow.

Christmas is coming, time to place the orders for oysters and *foie gras* and fresh black truffles. Time to promise ourselves that this year we will definitely go to the living *crèche* at the church in Ménerbes. It takes place at midnight, if Monsieur Poncet and his ass have arrived, and providing a suitably tractable baby Jesus has been discovered among the newly born inhabitants of the village. For three years, we have had every intention of going, and for three years we have been ambushed by dinner and the warmth of the wood fire. Full and sleepy, we have poked our noses out into the cold, looked at the Christmas tree of stars in the sky and thought how lucky we are to live here. It will probably be the same again this year.

Peter Mayle
December, 1989

JANUARY

The year began with lunch.

We have always found that New Year's Eve, with its eleventh-hour excesses and doomed resolutions, is a dismal occasion for all the forced jollity and midnight toasts and kisses. And so, when we heard that over in the village of Lacoste, a few miles away, the proprietor of Le Simiane was offering a six-course lunch with pink champagne to his amiable clientele, it seemed like a much more cheerful way to start the next twelve months.

By 12.30 the little stone-walled restaurant was full. There were some serious stomachs to be seen – entire families with the *embonpoint* that comes from spending two or three diligent hours every day at the table, eyes down and conversation postponed in the observance of France's favourite ritual. The proprietor of the restaurant, a man who had somehow perfected the art of hovering despite his considerable size, was dressed for the day in a velvet smoking jacket and bow tie. His moustache, sleek with pomade, quivered with enthusiasm as he rhapsodised over the menu: foie

1

gras, lobster mousse, beef *en croûte*, salads dressed in virgin oil, hand-picked cheeses, desserts of a miraculous lightness, *digestifs*. It was a gastronomic aria which he performed at each table, kissing the tips of his fingers so often that he must have blistered his lips.

The final '*bon appétit*' died away and a companionable near-silence descended on the restaurant as the food received its due attention. While we ate, my wife and I thought of previous New Year's Days, most of them spent under impenetrable cloud in England. It was hard to associate the sunshine and dense blue sky outside with the first of January but, as everyone kept telling us, it was quite normal. After all, we were in Provence.

We had been here often before as tourists, desperate for our annual ration of two or three weeks of true heat and sharp light. Always when we left, with peeling noses and regret, we promised ourselves that one day we would live here. We had talked about it during the long grey winters and the damp green summers, looked with an addict's longing at photographs of village markets and vineyards, dreamed of being woken up by the sun slanting through the bedroom window. And now, somewhat to our surprise, we had done it. We had committed ourselves. We had bought a house, taken French lessons, said our goodbyes, shipped over our two dogs and become foreigners.

In the end, it had happened quickly – almost impulsively – because of the house. We saw it one afternoon and had mentally moved in by dinner.

It was set above the country road that runs between the two mediaeval hill villages of Ménerbes and Bonnieux, at the end of a dirt track through cherry trees and vines. It was a *mas*, or farmhouse, built from local stone which two hundred years of wind and sun had weathered to a colour somewhere between pale honey and pale grey. It had started life in the eighteenth century as one room and, in the haphazard manner of agricultural buildings, had spread to accommodate children, grandmothers, goats and farm implements until it had become an irregular three-storey house. Everything about it was solid. The spiral staircase which rose from the wine *cave* to the top floor was cut from massive slabs of stone. The walls, some of them a metre thick, were built to keep out the winds of the Mistral which, they say, can blow the ears off a donkey. Attached to the back of the house was an enclosed courtyard, and beyond that a bleached white stone swimming pool. There were three wells, there were established shade trees and slim green cypresses, hedges of rosemary, a giant almond tree. In the afternoon sun, with the wooden shutters half-closed like sleepy eyelids, it was irresistible.

It was also immune, as much as any house could be, from the creeping horrors of property development. The French have a weakness for erecting *jolies villas* wherever building regulations permit, and sometimes where they don't, particularly in areas of hitherto unspoiled and beautiful countryside. We had seen them in a ghastly rash around the old market town of Apt, boxes made from that special kind of livid pink cement which remains livid no matter what the weather may throw at it. Very few areas of rural France are safe unless they have been officially protected, and one of the great attractions of this house was that it sat within the boundaries of a National Park, sacred to the French heritage and out of bounds to concrete-mixers.

The Lubéron mountains rise up immediately behind the house to a high point of nearly 3,500 feet and run in deep folds for about forty miles from west to east. Cedars and pines and scrub oak keep them perpetually green and provide cover for boar, rabbits and game birds. Wild flowers, thyme, lavender and mushrooms grow between the rocks and under the trees, and from the summit on a clear day the view is of the Basses-Alpes on one side and the Mediterranean on the other. For most of the year, it is possible to walk for eight or nine hours without seeing a car or a human being. It is a 247,000-acre extension of the back garden, a paradise for the dogs and a permanent barricade against assault from the rear by unforeseen neighbours.

Neighbours, we have found, take on an importance in the country that they don't begin to have in cities. You can live for years in an apartment in London or New York and barely speak to the people who live six inches away from you on the other side of a wall. In the country, separated from the next house though you may be by hundreds of yards, your neighbours are part of your life, and you are part of theirs. If you happen to be foreign and therefore slightly exotic, you are inspected with more than usual interest. And if, in addition, you inherit a long-standing and delicate agricultural arrangement, you are quickly made aware that your attitudes and decisions have a direct effect on another family's well-being.

We had been introduced to our new neighbours by the couple from whom we bought the house, over a five-hour dinner marked by a tremendous goodwill on all sides and an almost total lack of comprehension on our part. The language spoken was French, but it was not the French we had studied in textbooks and heard on cassettes; it was a rich, soupy patois, emanating from somewhere at the back of the throat and passing through a scrambling process in the nasal passages before coming out as speech. Half-familiar sounds could be dimly recognised as words through the swirls and eddies of Provençal: *demain* became *demang, vin* became *vang, maison* became *mesong*. That by itself would not have been a problem had the words been spoken at normal conversational speed and without further embroidery, but they were delivered like bullets from a machine-gun, often with an extra vowel tacked on to the end for good luck. Thus an offer of more bread – page one stuff in French for beginners – emerged as a single twanging question. *Encoredupanga?*

Fortunately for us, the good humour and niceness of our neighbours were apparent even if what they were saying was a mystery. Henriette was a brown, pretty woman with a permanent smile and a sprinter's enthusiasm for reaching the finishing line of each sentence in record time. Her husband Faustin – or Faustang, as we thought his name was spelt for many weeks – was large and gentle, unhurried in his movements and relatively slow with his words. He had been born in the valley, he had spent his life in the valley, and he would die in the valley. His father, Pépé André, who lived next to him, had shot his last boar at the age of eighty and had given up hunting to take up the bicycle. Twice a week he would pedal to the village for his groceries and his gossip. They seemed to be a contented family.

They had, however, a concern about us, not only as neighbours but as prospective partners, and, through the fumes of *marc* and black tobacco and the even thicker fog of the accent, we eventually got to the bottom of it.

Most of the six acres of land we had bought with the house was planted with vines, and these had been looked after for years under the traditional system of *métayage*: the owner of the land pays the capital costs of new vine stock and fertiliser, while the farmer does the work of spraying, cropping and pruning. At the end of the season, the farmer takes two-thirds of the profits and the owner one-third. If the property changes hands, the arrangement comes up for review, and there was Faustin's concern. It was well known that many of the properties in the Lubéron were bought as *résidences secondaires*, used for holidays and amusement, their good agricultural land turned into elaborately planted gardens. There were even cases of the ultimate blasphemy, when vines had been grubbed up to make way for tennis courts. Tennis courts! Faustin shrugged with disbelief, shoulders and eyebrows going up in unison as he contemplated the extraordinary idea of exchanging

5

precious vines for the curious pleasures of chasing a little ball around in the heat.

He needn't have worried. We loved the vines – the ordered regularity of them against the sprawl of the mountain, the way they changed from bright green to darker green to yellow and red as spring and summer turned to autumn, the blue smoke in the pruning season as the clippings were burned, the pruned stumps studding the bare fields in the winter – they were meant to be here. Tennis courts and landscaped gardens weren't. (Nor, for that matter, was our swimming pool, but at least it hadn't replaced any vines.) And, besides, there was the wine. We had the option of taking our profit in cash or in the bottle, and in an average year our share of the crop would be nearly a thousand litres of good ordinary red and pink. As emphatically as we could in our unsteady French, we told Faustin that we would be delighted to continue the existing arrangement. He beamed. He could see that we would all get along very well together. One day, we might even be able to talk to each other.

* * * * *

The proprietor of Le Simiane wished us a happy new year and hovered in the doorway as we stood in the narrow street, blinking into the sun.

'Not bad, eh?' he said, with a flourish of one velvet-clad arm which took in the village, the ruins of the Marquis de Sade's château perched above, the view across to the mountains and the bright, clean sky. It was a casually possessive gesture, as if he was showing us a corner of his personal estate. 'One is fortunate to be in Provence.'

Yes indeed, we thought, one certainly was. If this was winter we wouldn't be needing all the foul-weather paraphernalia – boots and coats and inch-thick sweaters – that we had brought over from England. We drove home, warm and well-fed, making bets on how soon we could take the first swim of the year, and feeling a smug sympathy for those poor souls in harsher climates who had to suffer real winters.

Meanwhile, a thousand miles to the north, the wind that had

started in Siberia was picking up speed for the final part of its journey. We had heard stories about the Mistral. It drove people, and animals, mad. It was an extenuating circumstance in crimes of violence. It blew for fifteen days on end, uprooting trees, overturning cars, smashing windows, tossing old ladies into the gutter, splintering telegraph poles, moaning through houses like a cold and baleful ghost, causing *la grippe*, domestic squabbles, absenteeism from work, toothache, migraine – every problem in Provence that couldn't be blamed on the politicians was the fault of the *sâcré vent* which the Provençaux spoke about with a kind of masochistic pride.

Typical Gallic exaggeration, we thought. If they had to put up with the gales that come off the English Channel and bend the rain so that it hits you in the face almost horizontally, then they might know what a real wind was like. We listened to their stories and, to humour the tellers, pretended to be impressed.

And so we were poorly prepared when the first Mistral of the year came howling down the Rhône valley, turned left and smacked into the west side of the house with enough force to skim roof tiles into the swimming pool and rip a window that had carelessly been left open off its hinges. The temperature dropped 20 degrees in twenty-four hours. It went to zero, then six below. Readings taken in Marseille showed a wind speed of 180 kilometres an hour. My wife was cooking in an overcoat. I was trying to type in gloves. We stopped talking about our first swim and thought wistfully about central heating. And then one morning, with the sound of branches snapping, the pipes burst one after the other under the pressure of water that had frozen in them overnight.

They hung off the wall, swollen and stopped up with ice, and Monsieur Menicucci studied them with his professional plumber's eye.

'*Oh là là,*' he said. '*Oh là là.*' He turned to his young apprentice, whom he invariably addressed as *jeune homme* or *jeune*. 'You see what we have here, *jeune*. Naked pipes. No insulation. Côte d'Azur plumbing. In Cannes, in Nice, it would do, but here . . .'

He made a clucking sound of disapproval and wagged his finger under *jeune*'s nose to underline the difference between the soft winters of the coast and the biting cold in which we were now standing, and pulled his woollen bonnet firmly down over his ears. He was short and compact, built for plumbing, as he would say, because he could squeeze himself into constricted spaces that more ungainly men would find inaccessible. While we waited for *jeune* to set up the blowlamp, Monsieur Menicucci delivered the first of a series of lectures and collected *pensées* which I would listen to with increasing enjoyment throughout the coming year. Today, we had a geophysical dissertation on the increasing severity of Provençal winters.

For three years in a row, winters had been noticeably harder than anyone could remember – cold enough, in fact, to kill ancient olive trees. It was, to use the phrase that comes out in Provence whenever the sun goes in, *pas normale*. But why? Monsieur Menicucci gave me a token two seconds to ponder this phenomenon before warming to his thesis, tapping me with a finger from time to time to make sure I was paying attention.

It was clear, he said, that the winds which brought the cold down from Russia were arriving in Provence with greater velocity than before, taking less time to reach their destination and therefore having less time to warm up en route. And the reason for this – Monsieur Menicucci allowed himself a brief but dramatic pause – was a change in the configuration of the earth's crust. *Mais oui.* Somewhere between Siberia and Ménerbes the curvature of the earth had flattened, enabling the wind to take a more direct route south. It was entirely logical. Unfortunately, part two of the lecture (Why The Earth Is Becoming Flatter) was interrupted by a crack of another burst pipe, and my education was put aside for some virtuoso work with the blow-lamp.

The effect of the weather on the inhabitants of Provence is immediate and obvious. They expect every day to be sunny, and their disposition suffers when it isn't. Rain they take as a personal affront, shaking their heads and commiserating with each other in the cafés, looking with profound suspicion at the sky as though a plague of locusts is about to descend and picking their way with distaste through the puddles on the pavement. If anything worse than a rainy day should come along, such as this sub-zero snap, the result is startling: most of the population disappears.

8

As the cold began to bite into the middle of January, the towns and villages became quiet. The weekly markets, normally jammed and boisterous, were reduced to a skeleton crew of intrepid stallholders who were prepared to risk frostbite for a living, stamping their feet and nipping from hip flasks. Customers moved briskly, bought and went, barely pausing to count their change. Bars closed their doors and windows tight and conducted their business in a pungent fug. There was none of the usual dawdling on the streets.

Our valley hibernated, and I missed the sounds which marked the passing of each day almost as precisely as a clock: Faustin's rooster having his morning cough; the demented clatter – like nuts and bolts trying to escape from a biscuit tin – of the small Citroën van that every farmer drives home at lunchtime; the hopeful fusillade of a hunter on afternoon patrol in the vines on the opposite hillside; the distant whine of a chainsaw in the forest; the twilight serenade of farm dogs. Now there was silence. For hours on end the valley would be completely still and empty, and we became curious. What was everybody doing?

Faustin, we knew, travelled round the neighbouring farms as a visiting slaughterer, slitting the throats and breaking the necks of rabbits and ducks and pigs and geese so that they could be turned into terrines and hams and *confits*. We thought it an uncharacteristic occupation for a soft-hearted man who spoilt his dogs, but he was evidently skilled and quick and, like any true countryman, he wasn't distracted by sentiment. We might treat a rabbit as a pet or become emotionally attached to a goose, but we had come from cities and supermarkets, where flesh was hygienically distanced from any resemblance to living creatures. A shrink-wrapped pork chop has a sanitised, abstract appearance that has nothing whatever to do with the warm, mucky bulk of a pig. Out here in the country there was no avoiding the direct link between death and dinner, and there would be many occasions in the future when we would be grateful for Faustin's winter work.

But what did everyone else do? The earth was frozen, the vines were clipped and dormant, it was too cold to hunt. Had they all gone on holiday? No, surely not. These were not the kind of gentlemen farmers who spent their winters on the ski slopes or yachting in the Caribbean. Holidays here were taken at home during August, eating too much, enjoying siestas and resting up before the long days of the *vendange*. It was a puzzle, until we realised how many of the local people had their birthdays in September or October, and then a possible but unverifiable answer suggested itself: they were busy indoors making babies. There is a season for everything in Provence, and the first two months of the year must be devoted to procreation. We have never dared ask.

The cold weather brought less private pleasures. Apart from the peace and emptiness of the landscape, there is a special smell about winter in Provence which is accentuated by the wind and the clean, dry air. Walking in the hills, I was often able to smell a house before I could see it, because of the scent of woodsmoke coming from an invisible chimney. It is one of the most primitive smells in life, and consequently extinct in most cities, where fire regulations and interior decorators have combined to turn fireplaces into blocked-up holes or self-consciously lit 'architectural features'. The fireplace in Provence is still used – to cook on, to sit round, to warm the toes and please the eye – and fires are laid in the early morning and fed throughout the day with scrub oak from the Lubéron or beech from the foothills of Mont Ventoux. Coming home with the dogs as dusk fell, I always stopped to look from the top of the valley at the long zig-zag of smoke ribbons drifting up from the farms that are scattered along the Bonnieux road. It was a sight that made me think of warm kitchens and well-seasoned stews, and it never failed to make me ravenous.

The well-known food of Provence is summer food – the melons and peaches and asparagus, the courgettes and aubergines, the peppers and tomatoes, the *aioli* and bouillabaisse and monumental salads of olives and anchovies and tuna and hard-boiled eggs and sliced, earthy potatoes on beds of multicoloured lettuce glistening with oil, the fresh goats' cheeses – these had been the memories that came back to torment us every time we looked at the limp and shrivelled selection on offer in English shops. It had never occurred to us that there was a winter menu, totally different but equally delicious.

The cold weather cuisine of Provence is peasant food. It is made to stick to your ribs, keep you warm, give you strength and send you off to bed with a full belly. It is not pretty, in the way that the tiny and artistically garnished portions served in fashionable restaurants are pretty, but on a freezing night with the Mistral coming at you like a razor there is nothing to beat it. And on the night one of our neighbours invited us to dinner it was cold enough to turn the short walk to their house into a short run.

We came through the door and my glasses steamed up in the heat from the fireplace that occupied most of the far wall of the room. As the mist cleared, I saw that the big table, covered in checked oilcloth, was laid for ten; friends and relations were coming to examine us. A television set chattered in the corner, the radio chattered back from the kitchen, and assorted dogs and cats were shooed out of the door as one guest arrived, only to sidle back in with the next. A tray of drinks was brought out, with pastis for the men and chilled, sweet muscat wine for the women, and we were caught in a crossfire of noisy complaints about the weather. Was it as bad as this in England? Only in the summer, I said. For a moment they took me seriously before someone saved me from embarrassment by laughing. With a great deal of jockeying for position – whether to sit next to us or as far away as possible, I wasn't sure – we settled ourselves at the table.

It was a meal that we shall never forget; more accurately, it was several meals that we shall never forget, because it went beyond the gastronomic frontiers of anything we had ever experienced, both in quantity and length.

It started with home-made pizza – not one, but three: anchovy, mushroom and cheese, and it was obligatory to have a slice of each. Plates were then wiped with pieces torn from the two-foot loaves in the middle of the table, and the next course came out. There were pâtés of rabbit, boar and thrush. There was a chunky, pork-based terrine laced with *marc*. There were *saucissons* spotted with peppercorns. There were tiny sweet onions marinated in a fresh tomato sauce. Plates were wiped once more and duck was brought in. The slivers of *magret* that appear, arranged in fan formation and lapped by an elegant smear of sauce on the refined tables of nouvelle cuisine – these were nowhere to be seen. We had entire breasts, entire legs, covered in a dark, savoury gravy and surrounded by wild mushrooms.

We sat back, thankful that we had been able to finish, and watched with something close to panic as plates were wiped yet again and a huge, steaming casserole was placed on the table. This was the speciality of Madame our hostess – a rabbit *civet* of the richest, deepest brown – and our feeble requests for small portions were smilingly ignored. We ate it. We ate the green salad with knuckles of bread fried in garlic and olive oil, we ate the plump round *crottins* of goat's cheese, we ate the almond and cream gâteau that the daughter of the house had prepared. That night, we ate for England.

With the coffee, a number of deformed bottles were produced which contained a selection of locally-made *digestifs*. My heart would have sunk had there been any space left for it to sink to, but there was no denying my host's insistence. I must try one particular concoction, made from an eleventh-century recipe by an alcoholic order of monks in the Basses-Alpes. I was asked to close my eyes while it was poured, and when I opened them a tumbler of viscous yellow fluid had been put in front of me. I looked in despair round the table. Everyone was watching me; there was no chance of giving whatever it was to the dog or letting it dribble discreetly into one of my shoes. Clutching the table for support with one hand, I took the tumbler with the other, closed my eyes, prayed to the patron saint of indigestion, and threw it back.

Nothing came out. I had been expecting at best a scalded tongue, at worst permanently cauterised taste buds, but I took in nothing but air. It was a trick glass, and for the first time in my adult life I was deeply relieved not to have a drink. As the laughter of the other guests died away, genuine drinks were threatened, but we were saved by the cat. From her headquarters on top of a large *armoire*, she took a flying leap in pursuit of a moth and crash-landed among the coffee cups and bottles on the table. It seemed like an appropriate moment to leave. We walked home pushing our stomachs before us, oblivious to the cold, incapable of speech, and slept like the dead.

Even by Provençal standards, it had not been an everyday meal. The people who work on the land are more likely to eat well at noon and sparingly in the evening, a habit which is healthy and sensible and, for us, quite impossible. We have found that there is nothing like a good lunch to give us an appetite for dinner. It's alarming. It must have something to do with the novelty of living in the middle of such an abundance of good things to eat, and among men and women whose interest in food verges on obsession. Butchers, for instance, are not content merely to sell you meat. They will tell you, at great length, while the queue backs up behind you, how to cook it, how to serve it and what to eat and drink with it.

The first time this happened, we had gone into Apt to buy veal for the Provençal stew called *pebronata*. We were directed towards a butcher in the old part of town who was reputed to have the master's touch and to be altogether *très sérieux*. His shop was small, he and his wife were large, and the four of us constituted a crowd. He listened intently as we explained that we wanted to make this particular dish; perhaps he had heard of it.

He puffed up with indignation, and began to sharpen a large

knife so energetically that we stepped back a pace. Did we realise, he said, that we were looking at an expert, possibly the greatest *pebronata* authority in the Vaucluse? His wife nodded admiringly. Why, he said, brandishing ten inches of sharp steel in our faces, he had written a book about it – a *definitive* book – containing twenty variations of the basic recipe. His wife nodded again. She was playing the rôle of senior nurse to his eminent surgeon, passing him fresh knives to sharpen prior to the operation.

We must have looked suitably impressed, because he then produced a handsome piece of veal and his tone became prof-essorial. He trimmed the meat, cubed it, filled a small bag with chopped herbs, told us where to go to buy the best peppers (four green and one red, the contrast in colour being for aesthetic reasons), went through the recipe twice to make sure we weren't going to commit a *bêtise* and suggested a suitable Côtes du Rhône. It was a fine performance.

Gourmets are thick on the ground in Provence, and pearls of wisdom have sometimes come from the most unlikely sources. We were getting used to the fact that the French are as passionate about food as other nationalities are about sport and politics, but even so it came as a surprise to hear Monsieur Bagnols the floor-cleaner handicapping three-star restaurants. He had come over from Nîmes to sand down a stone floor, and it was apparent from the start that he was not a man who trifled with his stomach. Each day precisely at noon he changed out of his overalls and took himself off to one of the local restaurants for two hours.

He judged it to be not bad, but of course nothing like the Beaumanière at Les Baux. The Beaumanière has three Michelin stars and a 17 out of 20 rating in the Gault-Millau Guide and there, he said, he had eaten a truly exceptional sea bass *en croûte*. Mind you, the Troisgros in Roanne was a superb establishment too, although being opposite the station the setting wasn't as pretty as Les Baux. The Troisgros has three Michelin stars and a 19½ out of 20 rating in the Gault-Millau Guide. And so it went on, as he adjusted his knee pads and scrubbed away at the floor, a personal guide to five or six of the most expensive restaurants in France that Monsieur Bagnols had visited on his annual treats.

He had once been in England, and had eaten roast lamb at a

hotel in Liverpool. It had been grey and tepid and tasteless. But of course, he said, it is well known that the English kill their lamb twice; once when they slaughter it, and once when they cook it. I retreated in the face of such withering contempt for my national cuisine, and left him to get on with the floor and dream of his next visit to Bocuse.

* * * * *

The weather continued hard, with bitter but extravagantly starry nights and spectacular sunrises. One early morning, the sun seemed abnormally low and large, and walking into it everything was either glare or deep shadow. The dogs were running well ahead of me, and I heard them barking long before I could see what they had found.

We had come to a part of the forest where the land fell away to form a deep bowl in which, a hundred years before, some misguided farmer had built a house that was almost permanently in the gloom cast by the surrounding trees. I had passed it many times. The windows were always shuttered, and the only sign of human habitation was smoke drifting up from the chimney. In the yard outside, two large and matted Alsatians and a black mongrel were constantly on the prowl, howling and straining against their chains in their efforts to savage any passers-by. These dogs were known to be vicious; one of them had broken loose and laid open the back of grandfather André's leg. My dogs, full of valour when confronted by timid cats, had wisely decided against passing too close to three sets of hostile jaws, and had developed the habit of making a detour round the house and over a small steep hill. They were at the top now, barking in that speculative, nervous manner that dogs adopt to reassure themselves when they encounter something unexpected in familiar territory.

I reached the top of the hill with the sun full in my eyes, but I could make out the back-lit silhouette of a figure in the trees, a nimbus of smoke around his head, the dogs inspecting him noisily from a safe distance. As I came up to him, he extended a cold, horny hand.

'Bon jour.' He unscrewed a cigarette butt from the corner of his mouth and introduced himself. 'Massot, Antoine.'

He was dressed for war. A stained camouflage jacket, an army jungle cap, a bandolier of cartridges and a pump-action shotgun. His face was the colour and texture of a hastily cooked steak, with a wedge of nose jutting out above a ragged, nicotine-stained moustache. Pale blue eyes peered through a sprouting tangle of ginger eyebrows, and his decayed smile would have brought despair to the most optimistic dentist. Nevertheless, there was a certain mad amiability about him.

I asked if his hunting had been successful. 'A fox,' he said, 'but too old to eat.' He shrugged, and lit another of his fat Boyards cigarettes, wrapped in yellow maize paper and smelling like a young bonfire in the morning air. 'Anyway,' he said, 'he won't be keeping my dogs awake at night,' and he nodded down towards the house in the hollow.

I said that his dogs seemed fierce, and he grinned. Just playful, he said. But what about the time one of them had escaped and attacked the old man? Ah, that. He shook his head at the painful memory. The trouble is, he said, you should never turn your back on a playful dog, and that had been the old man's mistake. *Une vraie catastrophe*. For a moment, I thought he was regretting the wound inflicted on grandfather André, which had punctured a vein in his leg and required a visit to the hospital for injections and stitches, but I was mistaken. The real sadness was that Massot had been obliged to buy a new chain, and those robbers in Cavaillon had charged him 250 francs. That had bitten deeper than teeth.

To save him further anguish, I changed the subject and asked him if he really ate fox. He seemed surprised at such a stupid question, and looked at me for a moment or two without replying, as though he suspected me of making fun of him.

'One doesn't eat fox in England?' I had visions of the members of the Belvoir Hunt writing to *The Times* and having a collective heart attack at such an unsporting and typically foreign idea.

'No, one doesn't eat fox in England. One dresses up in a red coat and one chases after it on horseback with several dogs, and then one cuts off its tail.'

He cocked his head, astonished. *'Ils sont bizarres, les Anglais.'* And then, with great gusto and some hideously explicit gestures, he described what civilised people did with a fox.

Civet de renard à la façon Massot

Find a young fox, and be careful to shoot it cleanly in the head, which is of no culinary interest. Buckshot in the edible parts of the fox can cause chipped teeth – Massot showed me two of his – and indigestion.

Skin the fox, and cut off its *parties*. Here, Massot made a chopping motion with his hand across his groin, and followed this with some elaborate twists and tugs of the hand to illustrate the gutting process.

Leave the cleaned carcass under cold running water for 24 hours to eliminate the *goût sauvage*. Drain it, bundle it up in a sack and hang it outdoors overnight, preferably when there is frost.

The following morning, place the fox in a casserole of cast iron and cover with a mixture of blood and red wine. Add herbs, onions and heads of garlic, and simmer for a day or two. (Massot apologised for his lack of precision but said that the timing varied according to size and age of fox.)

In the old days, this was eaten with bread and boiled potatoes, but now, thanks to progress and the invention of the deep-fat fryer, one could enjoy it with *pommes frites*.

By now, Massot was in a talkative mood. He lived alone, he told me, and company was scarce in the winter. He had spent his life in the mountains, but maybe it was time to move into the village, where he could be among people. Of course, it would be a tragedy to leave such a beautiful house, so calm, so sheltered from the Mistral, so perfectly situated to escape the heat of the midday sun, a place where he had passed so many happy years. It would break his heart, unless – he looked at me closely, pale eyes watery with sincerity – unless he could render me a service by making it possible for one of my friends to buy his house.

I looked down at the ramshackle building huddled in the shadows, with the three dogs padding endlessly to and fro on their rusting chains, and thought that in the whole of Provence it would be difficult to find a less appealing spot to live. There was no sun, no view, no feeling of space, and almost certainly, a dank and horrid interior. I promised Massot that I would bear it in mind, and he winked at me. 'A million francs,' he said. 'A sacrifice.' And in the meantime, until he left this little corner of paradise, if there was anything I wanted to know about the rural life, he would advise me. He knew every centimetre of the forest, where the mushrooms grew, where the wild boar came to drink, which gun to choose, how to train a hound – there was nothing he didn't know, and this knowledge was mine for the asking. I thanked him. '*C'est normale*,' he said, and stumped off down the hill to his million-franc residence.

* * * * *

When I told a friend in the village that I had met Massot, he smiled.

'Did he tell you how to cook a fox?'

I nodded.

'Did he try to sell his house?'

I nodded.

'The old *blagueur*. He's full of wind.'

I didn't care. I liked him, and I had a feeling that he would be a rich source of fascinating and highly suspect information. With him to initiate me into the joys of rustic pursuits and Monsieur Menicucci in charge of more scientific matters, all I needed now was a navigator to steer me through the murky waters of French bureaucracy, which in its manifold subtleties and inconveniences can transform a molehill of activity into a mountain of frustration.

We should have been warned by the complications attached to the purchase of the house. We wanted to buy, the proprietor wanted to sell, a price was agreed, it was all straightforward. But then we became reluctant participants in the national sport of paper-gathering. Birth certificates were required to prove we existed; passports to prove that we were British; marriage certificates to enable us to buy the house in our joint names; divorce certificates to prove that our marriage certificates were valid; proof that we had an address in England (our driver's licences, plainly addressed, were judged to be insufficient; did we have more formal evidence of where we were living, like an old electricity bill?). Back

and forth between France and England the pieces of paper went –
every scrap of information except blood type and fingerprints –
until the local lawyer had our lives contained in a dossier. The
transaction could then proceed.

We made allowances for the system because we were foreigners
buying a tiny part of France, and national security clearly had to be
safeguarded. Less important business would doubtless be quicker
and less demanding of paperwork. We went to buy a car.

It was the standard Citroën *deux chevaux*, a model which has
changed very little in the past twenty-five years. Consequently,
spare parts are available in every village. Mechanically it is not
much more complicated than a sewing machine, and any reason-
ably competent blacksmith can repair it. It is cheap, and has a
comfortingly low top speed. Apart from the fact that the suspension is made of blancmange, which makes it the only car in the
world likely to cause sea-sickness, it is a charming and practical
vehicle. And the garage had one in stock.

The salesman looked at our driver's licences, valid throughout
the countries of the Common Market until well past the year 2000.
With an expression of infinite regret, he shook his head and looked
up.

'*Non.*'

'*Non?*'

'*Non.*'

We produced our secret weapons: two passports.

'*Non.*'

We rummaged around in our papers. What could he want? Our
marriage certificate? An old English electricity bill? We gave up,
and asked him what else, apart from money, was needed to buy a
car.

'You have an address in France?'

We gave it to him, and he noted it down on the sales form with
great care, checking from time to time to make sure that the third
carbon copy was legible.

'You have proof that this is your address? A telephone bill? An
electricity bill?'

We explained that we hadn't yet received any bills because we
had only just moved in. He explained that an address was

necessary for the *carte grise* – the document of car ownership. No address, no *carte grise*. No *carte grise*, no car.

Fortunately, his salesman's instincts overcame his relish for a bureaucratic impasse, and he leaned forward with a solution: if we would provide him with the deed of sale of our house, the whole affair could be brought to a swift and satisfactory conclusion, and we could have the car. The deed of sale was in the lawyer's office, fifteen miles away. We went to get it, and placed it triumphantly on his desk, together with a cheque. Now could we have the car?

'*Malheureusement, non.*' We must wait until the cheque had been cleared, a delay of four or five days, even though it was drawn on a local bank. Could we go together to the bank and clear it immediately? No, we couldn't. It was lunchtime. The two areas of endeavour in which France leads the world – bureaucracy and gastronomy – had combined to put us in our place.

It made us mildly paranoid, and for weeks we never left home without photocopies of the family archives, waving passports and birth certificates at everyone from the check-out girl at the supermarket to the old man who loaded the wine into the car at the co-operative. The documents were always regarded with interest, because documents are holy things here and deserve respect, but we were often asked why we carried them around. Was this the way one was obliged to live in England? What a strange and tiresome country is must be. The only short answer to that was a shrug. We practised shrugging.

The cold lasted until the final days of January, and then turned perceptibly warmer. We anticipated spring, and I was anxious to hear an expert forecast. I decided to consult the sage of the forest.

Massot tugged reflectively at his moustache. There were signs, he said. Rats can sense the coming of warmer weather before any of those complicated satellites, and the rats in his roof had been unusually active these past few days. In fact, they had kept him awake one night and he had loosed off a couple of shots into the ceiling to quieten them down. *Eh, oui.* Also, the new moon was due, and that often brought a change at this time of year. Based on these two significant portents, he predicted an early, warm spring. I hurried home to see if there were any traces of blossom on the almond tree, and thought about cleaning the swimming pool.

FEBRUARY

The front page of our newspaper, *Le Provençal*, is usually devoted to the fortunes of local football teams, the windy pronouncements of minor politicians, breathless reports of supermarket hold-ups in Cavaillon – '*le Chicago de Provence*' – and the occasional ghoulish account of sudden death on the roads caused by drivers of small Renaults trying to emulate Alain Prost.

This traditional mixture was put aside, one morning in early February, for a lead story which had nothing to do with sport, crime or politics: PROVENCE UNDER BLANKET OF SNOW! shouted the headline with an undercurrent of glee at the promise of the follow-up stories which would undoubtedly result from nature's unseasonable behaviour. There would be mothers and babies miraculously alive after a night in a snowbound car, old men escaping hypothermia by inches thanks to the intervention of public-spirited and alert neighbours, climbers plucked from the side of Mont Ventoux by helicopter, postmen battling against all odds to deliver electricity bills, village elders harking back to previous catastrophes – there were days of material ahead, and the writer of that first story could almost be seen rubbing his hands in anticipation as he paused between sentences to look for some more exclamation marks.

Two photographs accompanied the festive text. One was of a line of white, feathery umbrellas – the snow-draped palm trees along the Promenade des Anglais in Nice. The other showed a muffled figure in Marseille dragging a mobile radiator on its wheels through the snow at the end of a rope, like a man taking an angular and obstinate dog for a walk. There were no pictures of the countryside under snow because the countryside was cut off; the nearest snowplough was north of Lyon, three hundred kilometres away, and to a Provençal motorist – even an intrepid journalist – brought up on the sure grip of baking tarmac, the horror of waltzing on ice was best avoided by staying home or holing up in the nearest bar. After all, it wouldn't be for long. This was an aberration, a short-lived climatic hiccup, an excuse for a second *café crème* and perhaps something a little stronger to get the heart started before venturing outside.

Our valley had been quiet during the cold days of January, but now the snow had added an extra layer of silence, as though the entire area had been soundproofed. We had the Lubéron to ourselves, eerie and beautiful, mile after mile of white icing marked only by occasional squirrel and rabbit tracks crossing the footpaths in straight and purposeful lines. There were no human footprints except ours. The hunters, so evident in warmer weather with their weaponry and their arsenals of salami, baguettes, beer, Gauloises and all the other necessities for a day out braving nature in the raw, had stayed in their burrows. The sounds we mistook for gun shots were branches snapping under the weight of great swags of snow. Otherwise it was so still that, as Massot observed later, you could have heard a mouse fart.

Closer to home, the drive had turned into a miniature mountainscape where wind had drifted the snow into a range of knee-deep mounds, and the only way out was on foot. Buying a loaf of bread became an expedition lasting nearly two hours – into Ménerbes and back without seeing a single moving vehicle, the white humps of parked cars standing as patiently as sheep by the side of the hill leading up to the village. The Christmas-card weather had infected the inhabitants, who were greatly amused by their own efforts to negotiate the steep and treacherous streets, either teetering precariously forward from the waist or leaning even more precariously backward, placing their feet with the awkward deliberation of intoxicated roller-skaters. The municipal cleaning squad, two men with brooms, had cleared the access routes to essential services – butcher, baker, *épicerie* and café – and small knots of villagers stood in the sunshine congratulating each other on their fortitude in the face of calamity. A man on skis appeared from the direction of the Mairie and, with marvellous inevitability, collided with the only other owner of assisted transport, a man on an ancient sled. It was a pity the journalist from *Le Provençal* wasn't there to see it: SNOW CLAIMS VICTIMS IN HEAD-ON COLLISION, he could have written, and he could have watched it all from the steamy comfort of the café.

The dogs adapted to the snow like young bears, plunging into the drifts to emerge with white whiskers and bucking their way across the fields in huge, frothy leaps. And they learned to skate. The pool, that just days before I had been planning to clean and make ready for some early spring swimming, was a block of blue-green ice, and it seemed to fascinate them. On to the ice would go the two front paws, then a tentative third paw, and finally the remaining leg would join the rest of the dog. There would be a moment or two of contemplation at the curiosity of a life in which you can drink something one day and stand on it the next before the tail would start whirring with excitement and a form of progress could be made. I had always thought that dogs were engineered on the principle of four-wheel drive vehicles, with equal propulsion coming from each leg, but the power appears to be concentrated in the back. Thus the front half of the skating dog may have the intention of proceeding in a straight line, but the rear half is wildly out of control, fishtailing from side to side and sometimes threatening to overtake.

The novelty of being marooned in the middle of a picturesque sea was, during the day, a great pleasure. We walked for miles, we chopped wood, we ate enormous lunches and we stayed warm. But at night, even with fires and sweaters and yet more food, the

23

chill came up from the stone floors and out of the stone walls, making the toes numb and the muscles tight with cold. We were often in bed by nine o'clock and often, in the early morning, our breath was visible in small clouds over the breakfast table. If the Menicucci theory was correct and we were living in a flatter world, all future winters were going to be like this. It was time to stop pretending we were in a sub-tropical climate and give in to the temptations of central heating.

I called Monsieur Menicucci, and he asked anxiously about my pipes. I told him they were holding up well. 'That pleases me,' he said, 'because it is minus five degrees, the roads are perilous and I am fifty-eight years old. I am staying at home.' He paused, then added, 'I shall play the clarinet.' This he did every day to keep his fingers nimble and to take his mind off the hurly-burly of plumbing, and it was with some difficulty that I managed to steer the conversation away from his thoughts on the baroque composers and towards the mundane subject of our cold house. Eventually, we agreed that I should pay him a visit as soon as the roads had cleared. He had all kinds of installations at his house, he said – gas, oil, electricity and, his latest acquisition, a revolving solar heating panel. He would show them all to me and I could also meet Madame his wife, who was an accomplished soprano. I was obviously going to have a musical time among the radiators and stopcocks.

The prospect of being warm made us think of summer, and we started to make plans for turning the enclosed courtyard at the back of the house into an open-air living room. There was already a barbecue and a bar at one end, but what it lacked was a large, solid, permanent table. As we stood in six inches of snow, we tried to picture lunchtime in mid-August, and traced on the flagstones a five-foot square, large enough to seat eight bronzed and barefooted people and with plenty of room in the middle for giant bowls of salad, pâtés and cheese, cold roasted peppers, olive bread and chilled bottles of wine. The Mistral gusted through the courtyard and obliterated the shape in the snow, but by then we had decided: the table would be square and the top a single slab of stone.

Like most people who come to the Lubéron, we had been impressed by the variety and versatility of the local stone. It can be *pierre froide* from the quarry at Tavel, a smooth, close-grained pale beige; it can be *pierre chaude* from Lacoste, a rougher, softer off-white, or it can be any one of twenty shades and textures in between. There is a stone for fireplaces, for swimming pools, for staircases, for walls and floors, for garden benches and kitchen sinks. It can be rough or polished, hard-edged or rolled, cut square or in voluptuous curves. It is used where, in Britain or America, a builder might use wood or iron or plastic. Its only disadvantage, as we were finding out, is that it is cold in winter.

What came as a real surprise was the price. Metre for metre, stone was cheaper than linoleum, and we were so delighted by this rather misleading discovery – having conveniently overlooked the cost of laying stone – that we decided to risk the elements and go to the quarry without waiting for spring. Friends had suggested a man called Pierrot at Lacoste, whose work was good and whose prices were correct. He was described to us as *un original*, a character, and a rendezvous was made with him for 8.30 in the morning, while the quarry would still be quiet.

We followed a signpost off the side road out of Lacoste and along a track through the scrub oak towards the open countryside. It didn't look like a light industrial zone, and we were just about to turn back when we nearly fell into it – a huge hole bitten out of the ground, littered with blocks of stone. Some were raw, some worked into tombstones, memorials, giant garden urns, winged angels with intimidating blind stares, small triumphal arches or stocky round columns. Tucked away in a corner was a hut, its windows opaque with years of quarry dust.

We knocked and went in, and there was Pierrot. He was shaggy, with a wild black beard and formidable eyebrows. A piratical man. He made us welcome, beating the top layer of dust from two chairs with a battered trilby hat which he then placed carefully over the telephone on the table.

'English, eh?'

We nodded, and he leant towards us with a confidential air.

'I have an English car, a vintage Aston Martin. *Magnifique.*'

He kissed the tips of his fingers, speckling his beard with white, and poked among the papers on his table, raising puffs from every pile. Somewhere there was a photograph.

The phone started to make gravelly noises. Pierrot rescued it from under his hat and listened with an increasingly serious face before putting the phone down.

'Another tombstone,' he said. 'It's this weather. The old ones can't take the cold.' He looked around for his hat, retrieved it from his head, and covered the phone again, hiding the bad news.

He returned to the business at hand. 'They tell me you want a table.'

I had made a detailed drawing of our table, marking all the measurements carefully in metres and centimetres. For someone with the artistic flair of a five-year-old, it was a masterpiece. Pierrot looked at it briefly, squinting at the figures, and shook his head.

'*Non*. For a piece of stone this size, it needs to be twice as thick. Also, your base would collapse – *pouf*! – in five minutes, because the top will weigh . . .' he scribbled some calculations on my drawing '. . . between three and four hundred kilos.' He turned the paper over, and sketched on the back. 'There. That's what you want.' He pushed the sketch across to us. It was much better than mine, and showed a graceful monolith; simple, square, well-proportioned. 'A thousand francs, including delivery.'

We shook hands on it, and I promised to come back later in the week with a cheque. When I did, it was at the end of a working day, and I found that Pierrot had changed colour. From the top of his trilby down to his boots he was stark white, dusted all over as though he had been rolling in confectioner's sugar, the only man I have ever seen who aged twenty-five years in the course of a working day. According to our friends, whose information I didn't entirely trust, his wife ran the vacuum cleaner over him every night when he came home, and all the furniture in his house, from armchairs to bidets, was made from stone.

At the time, it was easy enough to believe. Deep winter in Provence has a curiously unreal atmosphere, the combination of silence and emptiness creating the feeling that you are separated from the rest of the world, detached from normal life. We could imagine meeting trolls in the forest or seeing two-headed goats by the light of a full moon, and for us it was a strangely enjoyable contrast to the Provence we remembered from summer holidays. For others, winter meant boredom or depression, or worse; the suicide rate in the Vaucluse, so we were told, was the highest in France, and it became more than a statistic when we heard that a man who lived two miles from us had hanged himself one night.

A local death brings sad little announcements, which are posted in the windows of shops and houses. The church bell tolls, and a procession dressed with unfamiliar formality makes its slow way up to the cemetery, which is often one of the most commanding sites in the village. An old man explained why this was so. 'The dead get the best view,' he said, 'because they are there for such a long time.' He cackled so hard at his own joke that he had a coughing fit, and I was worried that his turn had come to join them. When I told him about the cemetery in California where you pay more for a tomb with a view than for more modest accommodation he was not at all surprised. 'There are always fools,' he said, 'dead or alive.'

Days passed with no sign of a thaw, but the roads were now showing strips of black where farmers and their tractors had cleared away the worst of the snow, making a single-lane passage through the drifts either side. This brought out a side of the French motorist that I had never expected to see; he displayed patience, or at least a kind of mulish obstinacy that was far removed from his customary Grand Prix behaviour behind the wheel. I saw it on the roads round the village. One car would be driving cautiously along the clear middle lane and would meet another coming from the opposite direction. They would stop, snout to snout. Neither would give way by reversing. Neither would pull over to the side and risk getting stuck in a drift. Glaring through the windscreens at each other, the drivers would wait in the hope that another car would come up behind them, which would constitute a clear case of *force majeure* and oblige the single car to back down so that superior numbers could proceed.

And so it was with a light foot on the accelerator that I went off to see Monsieur Menicucci and his treasure house of heating appliances. He met me at the entrance to his storeroom, woollen bonnet pulled down to cover his ears, scarf wound up to his chin, gloved, booted, the picture of a man who took the challenge of keeping warm as a scientific exercise in personal insulation. We exchanged politenesses about my pipes and his clarinet and he ushered me inside to view a meticulously arranged selection of

tubes and valves and squat, mysterious machines crouched in corners. Menicucci was a talking catalogue, reeling off heating coefficients and therms which were so far beyond me that all I could do was to nod dumbly at each new revelation.

At last the litany came to an end. '*Et puis voilà,*' said Menicucci, and looked at me expectantly, as though I now had the world of central heating at my fingertips, and could make an intelligent and informed choice. I could think of nothing to say except to ask him how he heated his own house.

'Ah,' he said, tapping his forehead in mock admiration, 'that is not a stupid thing to ask. What kind of meat does the butcher eat?' And, with that mystical question hanging unanswered in the air, we went next door to his house. It was undeniably warm, almost stuffy, and Monsieur Menicucci made a great performance of removing two or three outer layers of clothing, mopping his brow theatrically and adjusting his bonnet to expose his ears to the air.

He walked over to a radiator and patted it on the head. 'Feel that,' he said, 'cast iron, not like the *merde* they use for radiators nowadays. And the boiler – you must see the boiler. But *attention,*' he stopped abruptly and prodded me with his lecturer's finger, 'it is not French. Only the Germans and the Belgians know how to make boilers.' We went into the boiler room, and I dutifully admired the elderly, dial-encrusted machine which was puffing and snorting against the wall. 'This gives twenty-one degrees throughout the house, even when the temperature outside is minus six,' and he threw open the outside door to let in some minus six air on cue. He had the good instructor's gift for illustrating his remarks wherever possible with practical demonstration, as though he was talking to a particularly dense child. (In my case, certainly as far as plumbing and heating were concerned, this was quite justified.)

Having met the boiler, we went back to the house and met Madame, a diminutive woman with a resonant voice. Did I want a *tisane*, some almond biscuits, a glass of Marsala? What I really wanted was to see Monsieur Menicucci in his bonnet playing his clarinet, but that would have to wait until another day. Meanwhile, I had been given much to think about. As I left to go to the car, I looked up at the revolving solar heating apparatus on the roof and saw that it was frozen solid, and I had a sudden longing for a house full of cast iron radiators.

I arrived home to discover that a scale model of Stonehenge had been planted behind the garage. The table had arrived – five feet square, five inches thick, with a massive base in the form of a cross. The distance between where it had been delivered and where we wanted it to be was no more than fifteen yards, but it might as well have been fifty miles. The entrance to the courtyard was too narrow for any mechanical transport, and the high wall and tiled half-roof that made a sheltered area ruled out the use of a crane. Pierrot had told us that the table would weigh between six and eight hundred pounds. It looked heavier.

He called that evening.

'Are you pleased with the table?'

Yes, the table is wonderful, but there is a problem.

'Have you put it up yet?'

No, that's the problem. Did he have any helpful suggestions?

'A few pairs of arms,' he said. 'Think of the Pyramids.'

Of course. All we needed were fifteen thousand Egyptian slaves and it would be done in no time.

'Well, if you get desperate, I know the rugby team in Carcassonne.'

And with that he laughed and hung up.

We went to have another look at the monster, and tried to work out how many people would be needed to manhandle it into the courtyard. Six? Eight? It would have to be balanced on its side to pass through the doorway. We had visions of crushed toes and multiple hernias, and belatedly understood why the previous owner of the house had put a light, folding table in the place we had chosen for our monument. We took the only reasonable course of action open to us, and sought inspiration in front of the fire with a glass of wine. It was unlikely that anyone would steal the table overnight.

As it turned out, a possible source of help was not long in coming. Weeks before, we had decided to rebuild the kitchen, and had spent many enlightening hours with our architect as we were introduced to French building terminology, to *coffres* and *rehausses* and *faux-plafonds* and *vide-ordures*, to *plâtrage* and *dallage* and *poutrelles* and *coins perdus*. Our initial excitement had turned into anti-climax as the plans became more and more dog-eared and, for one reason or another, the kitchen remained untouched. Delays had been caused by the weather, by the plasterer going skiing, by the chief *maçon* breaking his arm playing football on a motor-bike, by the winter torpor of local suppliers. Our architect, an expatriate Parisian, had warned us that building in Provence was very similar to trench warfare, with long periods of boredom interrupted by bursts of violent and noisy activity, and we had so far experienced the first phase for long enough to look forward to the second.

The assault troops finally arrived, with a deafening clatter, while the morning was still hesitating between dawn and daylight. We went outside with bleary eyes to see what had fallen down, and could just make out the shape of a truck, spiked with scaffolding. A cheerful bellow came from the driver's seat.

'Monsieur Mayle?'

I told him he'd found the right house.

'Ah bon. On va attaquer la cuisine. Allez!'

The door opened, and a cocker spaniel jumped out, followed by three men. There was an unexpected whiff of aftershave as the chief *maçon* mangled my hand and introduced himself and his team: Didier, the lieutenant Eric and the junior, a massive young man called Claude. The dog, Pénélope, declared the site open by relieving herself copiously in front of the house, and battle commenced.

We had never seen builders work like this, Everything was done on the double: scaffolding was erected and a ramp of planks was built before the sun was fully up, the kitchen window and sink disappeared minutes later, and by ten o'clock we were standing in a fine layer of preliminary rubble as Didier outlined his plans for destruction. He was brisk and tough, with the cropped hair and straight back of a military man; I could see him as a drill instructor in the Foreign Legion, putting young layabouts through their paces until they whimpered for mercy. His speech was percussive, full of the onomatopoeic words like *tok* and *crak* and *boum* that the French like to use when describing any form of collision or breakage – and there was to be plenty of both. The ceiling was coming down, the floor was coming up and all the existing fittings

31

coming out. It was a gutting job, the entire kitchen to be evacuated – *chut!* – through the hole that used to be a window. A wall of polythene sheeting was nailed up to screen the area from the rest of the house, and domestic catering operations were transferred to the barbecue in the courtyard.

It was startling to see and hear the joyful ferocity with which the three masons pulverised everything within sledgehammer range. They thumped and whistled and sang and swore amid the falling masonry and sagging beams, stopping (with some reluctance, it seemed to me) at noon for lunch. This was demolished with the same vigour as a partition wall – not modest packets of sandwiches, but large plastic hampers filled with chickens and sausage and *choucroute* and salads and loaves of bread, with proper crockery and cutlery. None of them drank alcohol, to our relief. A tipsy mason nominally in charge of a forty-pound hammer was a frightening thought. They were dangerous enough sober.

Pandemonium resumed after lunch, and continued until nearly seven o'clock without any break. I asked Didier if he regularly worked a ten- or eleven-hour day. Only in the winter, he said. In the summer it was twelve or thirteen hours, six days a week. He was amused to hear about the English timetable of a late start and an early finish, with multiple tea breaks. '*Une petite journée*' was how he described it, and asked if I knew any English masons who would like to work with him, just for the experience. I couldn't imagine a rush of volunteers.

When the masons had gone for the day, we dressed for a picnic in the Arctic and started to prepare our first dinner in the temporary kitchen. There was a barbecue fireplace and a fridge. A sink and two gas rings were built into the back of the bar. It had all the basic requirements except walls, and with the temperature still below zero walls would have been a comfort. But the fire of vine clippings was burning brightly, the smell of lamb chops and rosemary was in the air, the red wine was doing noble work as a substitute for central heating, and we felt hardy and adventurous. This delusion lasted through dinner until it was time to go outside and wash the dishes.

* * * * *

The first true intimations of spring came not from early blossom or the skittish behaviour of the rats in Massot's roof, but from England. With the gloom of January behind them, people in London were making holiday plans, and it was astonishing how many of those plans included Provence. With increasing regularity, the phone would ring as we were sitting down to dinner – the caller having a cavalier disregard for the hour's time difference between France and England – and the breezy, half-remembered voice of a distant acquaintance would ask if we were swimming yet. We were always non-committal. It seemed unkind to spoil their illusions by telling them that we were sitting in a permafrost zone with the Mistral screaming through the hole in the kitchen wall and threatening to rip open the polythene sheet which was our only protection against the elements.

The call would continue along a course that quickly became predictable. First, we would be asked if we were going to be at home during Easter or May, or whichever period suited the caller. With that established, the sentence which we soon came to dread – 'We were thinking of coming down around then . . .' – would be delivered, and would dangle, hopeful and unfinished, waiting for a faintly hospitable reaction.

It was difficult to feel flattered by this sudden enthusiasm to see us, which had lain dormant during the years we had lived in England, and it was difficult to know how to deal with it. There is nothing quite as thick-skinned as the seeker after sunshine and free lodging; normal social sidesteps don't work. You're booked up that week? Don't worry – we'll come the week after. You have a house full of builders? We don't mind; we'll be out by the pool anyway. You've stocked the pool with barracuda and put a tank trap in the drive? You've become teetotal vegetarians? You suspect the dogs of carrying rabies? It didn't matter what we said; there was a refusal to take it seriously, a bland determination to overcome any feeble obstacle we might invent.

We talked about the threatened invasions to other people who had moved to Provence, and they had all been through it. The first summer, they said, is invariably hell. After that, you learn to say no. If you don't, you will find yourselves running a small and highly unprofitable hotel from Easter until the end of September.

Sound but depressing advice. We waited nervously for the next phone call.

* * * * *

Life had changed, and the masons had changed it. If we got up at 6.30 we could have breakfast in peace. Any later, and the sound effects from the kitchen made conversation impossible. One morning when the drills and hammers were in full song, I could see my wife's lips move, but no words were reaching me. Eventually she passed me a note: Drink your coffee before it gets dirty.

But progress was being made. Having reduced the kitchen to a shell, the masons started, just as noisily, to rebuild, bringing all their materials up the plank ramp and through a window-sized space ten feet above the ground. Their stamina was extraordinary, and Didier – half-man, half fork-lift truck – was somehow able to run up the bouncing ramp pushing a wheelbarrow of wet cement, a cigarette in one side of his mouth and breath enough to whistle out of the other. I shall never know how the three of them were able to work in a confined space, under cold and difficult conditions, and remain so resolutely good-humoured.

Gradually, the structure of the kitchen took shape and the follow-up squad came to inspect it and to coordinate their various contributions. There was Ramon the plasterer, with his plaster-covered radio and basketball boots, Mastorino the painter, Trufelli the tile-layer, Zanchi the carpenter, and the *chef-plombier* himself, with *jeune* two paces behind him on an invisible lead, Monsieur Menicucci. There were often six or seven of them all talking at once among the debris, arguing about dates and availabilities while Christian, the architect, acted as referee.

It occurred to us that, if this energy could be channelled for an hour or so, we had enough bodies and biceps to shift the stone table into the courtyard. When I suggested this, there was instant co-operation. Why not do it now, they said. Why not indeed? We clambered out of the kitchen window and gathered round the table, which was covered with a white puckered skin of frost. Twelve hands grasped the slab and twelve arms strained to lift it. There was not the slightest movement. Teeth were sucked thoughtfully, and everyone walked round the table looking at it until Menicucci put his finger on the problem. The stone is porous, he said. It is filled with water like a sponge. the water has frozen, the stone has frozen, the ground has frozen. V*oilà*! It is immovable. You must wait until it has thawed. There was some desultory talk about blow-lamps and crowbars, but Menicucci put a stop to that, dismissing it as *patati-patata*, which I took to mean nonsense. The group dispersed.

With the house full of noise and dust six days a week, the oasis of Sunday was even more welcome than usual. We could lie in until the luxurious hour of 7.30 before the dogs began agitating for a walk, we could talk to each other without having to go outside, and we could console ourselves with the thought that we were one week closer to the end of the chaos and disruption. What we couldn't do, because of the limited cooking facilities, was to celebrate Sunday as it should always be celebrated in France, with a long and carefully judged lunch. And so, using the temporary kitchen as an excuse, we leapt rather than fell into the habit of eating out on Sunday.

As an appetiser, we would consult the oracular books, and came to depend more and more on the Gault-Millau guide. The Michelin is invaluable, and nobody should travel through France without it, but it is confined to the bare bones of prices and grades and specialities. Gault-Millau gives you the flesh as well. It will tell you about the chef – if he's young, where he was trained; if he's established, whether he's resting on his past success or still trying hard. It will tell you about the chef's wife, whether she is welcoming or *glaciale*. It will give you some indication of the style of the restaurant, and if there's a view or a pretty terrace. It will comment on the service and the clientele, on the prices and the atmosphere. And, often in great detail, on the food and the wine list. It is not infallible, and it is certainly not entirely free from prejudice, but it is amusing and always interesting and, because it is written in colloquial French, good homework for novices in the language like us.

The 1987 guide lists 5,500 restaurants and hotels in a suitably orotund and well-stuffed volume, and picking through it we came across a local entry that sounded irresistible. It was a restaurant at

Lambesc, about half an hour's drive away. The chef was a woman, described as '*l'une des plus fameuses cuisinières de Provence*', her dining room was a converted mill, and her cooking was '*pleine de force et de soleil*'. That would have been enough of a recommendation in itself, but what intrigued us most was the age of the chef. She was eighty.

It was grey and windy when we arrived in Lambesc. We still suffered twinges of guilt if we stayed indoors on a beautiful day, but this Sunday was bleak and miserable, the streets smeared with old snow, the inhabitants hurrying home from the bakery with bread clutched to the chest and shoulders hunched against the cold. It was perfect lunch weather.

We were early, and the huge vaulted dining room was empty. It was furnished with handsome Provençal antiques, heavy and dark and highly polished. The tables were large and so well-spaced that they were almost remote from each other, a luxury usually reserved for grand and formal restaurants. The sound of voices and the clatter of saucepans came from the kitchen, and something smelt delicious, but we had obviously anticipated opening time by a few minutes. We started to tiptoe out to find a drink in a café.

'Who are you?' a voice said.

An old man had emerged from the kitchen and was peering at us, screwing up his eyes against the light coming through the door. We told him we'd made a reservation for lunch.

'Sit down, then. You can't eat standing up.' He waved airily at the empty tables. We sat down obediently, and waited while he came slowly over with two menus. He sat down with us.

'American? German?'

English.

'Good,' he said, 'I was with the English in the war.'

We felt that we had passed the first test. One more correct answer and we might be allowed to see the menus which the old man was keeping to himself. I asked him what he would recommend.

'Everything,' he said. 'My wife cooks everything well.'

He dealt the menus out and left us to greet another couple, and we dithered enjoyably between lamb stuffed with herbs, *daube*, veal with truffles and an unexplained dish called the *fantaisie du chef.* The old man came back and sat down, listened to the order and nodded.

'It's always the same,' he said. 'It's the men who like the *fantaisie.*'

I asked for a half-bottle of white wine to go with the first course, and some red to follow.

'No,' he said, 'you're wrong.' He told us what to drink, and it was a red Côtes du Rhône from Visan. Good wine and good women came from Visan, he said. He got up and fetched a bottle from a vast dark cupboard.

'There. You'll like that.' (Later, we noticed that everybody had the same wine on their table.)

He went off to the kitchen, the oldest head waiter in the world, to pass our order to perhaps the oldest practising chef in France. We thought we heard a third voice from the kitchen, but there were no other waiters, and we wondered how two people with a combined age of over 160 managed to cope with the long hours and hard work. And yet, as the restaurant became busier, there were no delays, no neglected tables. In his unhurried and stately way, the old man made his rounds, sitting down from time to time for a chat with his clients. When an order was ready, Madame would clang a bell in the kitchen and her husband would raise his eyebrows in pretended irritation. If he continued talking, the bell would clang again, more insistently, and off he would go, muttering '*j'arrive, j'arrive*'.

The food was everything the Gault-Millau guide had promised, and the old man had been right about the wine. We did like it. And, by the time he served the tiny rounds of goats' cheese marinated in herbs and olive oil, we had finished it. I asked for another half-bottle, and he looked at me disapprovingly.

'Who's driving?'

'My wife.'

He went again to the dark cupboard. 'There are no half-bottles,' he said, 'you can drink as far as here.' He drew an imaginary line with his finger half way down the new bottle.

The kitchen bell had stopped clanging and Madame came out, smiling and rosy-faced from the heat of the ovens, to ask us if we had eaten well. She looked like a woman of sixty. The two of them stood together, his hand on her shoulder, while she talked about the antique furniture, which had been her dowry, and he interrupted. They were happy with each other and they loved their work, and we left the restaurant feeling that old age might not be so bad after all.

* * * * *

Ramon the plasterer was lying on his back on a precarious platform, an arm's-length below the kitchen ceiling. I passed a beer up to him, and he leant sideways on one elbow to drink it. It looked like an uncomfortable position, either for drinking or working, but he said he was used to it.

'Anyway,' he said, 'you can't stand on the floor and throw stuff up. That one who did the ceiling of the Sistine Chapel – you know, that Italian – he must have been on his back for weeks.'

Ramon finished the beer, his fifth of the day, handed down the empty bottle, belched lightly and returned to his labours. He had a slow, rhythmical style, flicking the plaster on to the ceiling with his trowel and working it into a chunky smoothness with a roll of his wrist. He said that, when it was finished, it would look as though it had been there for a hundred years. He didn't believe in rollers or sprayers or instruments of any sort apart from his trowel and his eye for a line and a curve, which he said was infallible. One evening after he had gone I checked his surfaces with a spirit level. They were all true, and yet they were unmistakably the work of a hand rather than a machine. The man was an artist, and well worth his beer ration.

A breeze was coming through the hole in the kitchen wall, and it felt almost mild. I could hear something dripping. When I went outside I found that the seasons had changed. The stone table was oozing water, and spring had arrived.

* * * * *

MARCH

The almond tree was in tentative blossom. The days were longer, often ending with magnificent evenings of corrugated pink skies. The hunting season was over, with hounds and guns put away for six months. The vineyards were busy again as the well-organised farmers treated their vines and their more lackadaisical neighbours hurried to do the pruning they should have done in November. The people of Provence greeted spring with uncharacteristic briskness, as if nature had given everyone an injection of sap.

The markets changed abruptly. On the stalls, fishing tackle and ammunition belts and waterproof boots and long brushes with steel bristles for amateur chimney-sweeps were replaced by displays of ferocious-looking agricultural implements – machetes and grubbing tools, scythes and hoes with sharp curved prongs, spraying equipment that was guaranteed to bring the rain of death down on any weed or insect foolhardy enough to threaten the grapes. Flowers and plants and tiny new season vegetables were everywhere, and café tables and chairs sprouted on the pavements. There was a feeling of activity and purpose in the air, and one or two optimists were already buying espadrilles from the multi-coloured racks outside the shoe shops.

In contrast to this bustle, work on the house had come to a standstill. Following some primeval springtime urge, the builders had migrated, leaving us with some token sacks of plaster and piles of sand as proof of their intention to come back – one day – and finish what they had so nearly finished. The phenomenon of the vanishing builder is well known throughout the world, but in Provence the problem has its own local refinements and frustrations, and its own clearly defined seasons.

Three times a year, at Easter, August and Christmas, the owners of holiday homes escape from Paris and Zürich and Düsseldorf and London to come down for a few days or weeks of the simple country life. Invariably, before they come, they think of something that is crucial to the success of their holiday: a set of Courrèges bidets, a searchlight in the swimming pool, a re-tiled terrace, a new roof for the servants' quarters. How can they possibly enjoy their rustic interlude without these essentials? In panic, they telephone the local builders and craftsmen. Get it done – it *must* be done – before we arrive. Implicit in these urgent instructions is the understanding that generous payments will be forthcoming if the work is done at once. Speed is of the essence; money isn't.

It is too tempting to ignore. Everyone remembers when Mitter-rand first came to power; the rich went into financial paralysis, and sat on their cash. Building work was scarce in Provence then, and who knows when bad times might come again? So the jobs are accepted, and less clamorous clients suddenly find themselves with dormant concrete-mixers and forlorn, uncompleted rooms. Faced with this situation, there are two ways to respond. Neither of them will produce immediate results, but one way will reduce the frustration, and the other will add to it.

We tried both. To begin with, we made a conscious effort to become more philosophical in our attitude to time, to treat days and weeks of delays in the Provençal fashion – that is, to enjoy the sunshine and to stop thinking like city people. This month, next month, what's the difference? Have a pastis and relax. It worked well enough for a week or two, and then we noticed that the building materials at the back of the house were turning green with the first growth of spring weeds. We decided to change our tactics and get some firm dates out of our small and elusive team of workmen. It was an educational experience.

We learned that time in Provence is a very elastic commodity, even when it is described in clear and specific terms. *Un petit quart d'heure* means some time today. *Demain* means some time this week. And, the most elastic time segment of all, *une quinzaine* can mean three weeks, two months or next year, but never, ever does it mean fifteen days. We learned also to interpret the hand language that accompanies any discussion of deadlines. When a Provençal looks you in the eye and tells you that he will be hammering on your door ready to start work next Tuesday for certain, the behaviour of his hands is all-important. If they are still, or patting you reassuringly on the arm, you can expect him on Tuesday. If one hand is held out at waist height, palm downwards, and begins to rock from side to side, adjust the timetable to Wednesday or Thursday. If the rocking develops into an agitated waggle, he's really talking about next week or God knows when, depending on circumstances beyond his control. These unspoken disclaimers, which seem to be instinctive and therefore more revealing than speech, are occasionally reinforced by the magic word *normalement*, a supremely versatile escape clause worthy of an insurance policy. *Normalement* – providing it doesn't rain, providing the truck hasn't broken down, providing the brother-in-law hasn't borrowed the tool box – is the Provençal builder's equivalent of the fine print in a contract, and we came to regard it with infinite suspicion.

But, despite their genial contempt for punctuality and their absolute refusal to use the telephone to say when they were coming or when they weren't, we could never stay irritated with them for long. They were always disarmingly cheerful, they worked long and hard when they were with us, and their work was excellent. In the end, they were worth waiting for. And so, little by little, we reverted to being philosophical, and came to terms with the Provençal clock. From now on, we told ourselves, we would assume that nothing would be done when we expected it to be done; the fact that it happened at all would be enough.

* * * * *

Faustin was behaving curiously. For two or three days he had been clanking up and down on his tractor, towing a contraption of metal intestines which spewed fertiliser to either side as he passed between the rows of vines. He kept stopping to get off the tractor and walk over to a field, now empty and overgrown, which had been planted with melons. He studied the field from one end, remounted his tractor, sprayed some more vines, and returned to study the other end. He paced, he pondered, he scratched his head. When he went home for lunch, I walked down to see what it was he found so fascinating, but to me it looked like any other fallow melon field – a few weeds, some tatters of plastic left over from the strips that had protected last year's crop, half an acre of nothing. I wondered if Faustin suspected it of harbouring buried treasure, because we had already dug up two gold Napoleon coins nearer the house, and he had told us that there were probably more to be found. But peasants don't hide their gold in the middle of cultivated land when it can be squirrelled away more securely under the flagstones or down a well. It was odd.

He came visiting that evening with Henriette, looking unusually spruce and businesslike in his white shoes and orange shirt, and bearing jars of home made rabbit pâté. Half way through his first pastis, he leant forward confidentially. Did we know that the wine produced from our vineyards – Côtes du Lubéron – was about to be given *Appellation Contrôlée* status? He leant back, nodding slowly, and said '*Eh oui*' several times while we absorbed the news. Clearly, said Faustin, the wine would become more expensive and vineyard-owners would make more money. And, clearly, the more vines one has the more money one makes.

There was no arguing with that, so Faustin moved on to a second drink – he drank in an efficient, unobtrusive way, and always reached the bottom of his glass before I expected – and put forward his proposition. It seemed to him that our melon field could be more profitably employed. He inhaled some pastis while Henriette produced a document from her bag. It was a *droit d'implantation*, giving us the right to plant vines, a privilege accorded to us by the government itself. While we looked at the paper, Faustin demolished the nonsensical idea of continuing to grow melons, dismissing them with a wave of his glass as being too demanding in terms of time and water, and always vulnerable to attack by the wild boar who come down from the mountains in the summer. Only last year, Faustin's brother Jacky had lost a third of his melon crop. Eaten by the boars! The profit disappearing into a pig's belly! Faustin shook his head at the painful memory, and had to be revived by a third large pastis.

By chance, he said, he had made some calculations. Our field would accommodate 1,300 new vines in place of the tiresome melons. My wife and I looked at each other. We were equally fond of wine and Faustin, and he obviously had his heart set on progress and expansion. We agreed that the extra vines sounded like a good idea, but thought no more about it after he had left. Faustin is a ruminant among men, not given to hasty action, and in any case, nothing happens quickly in Provence. Perhaps next spring he would get round to it.

At seven o'clock the following morning, a tractor was ploughing up the melon field, and two days later the planting team arrived – five men, two women and four dogs, under the direction of the *chef des vignes* Monsieur Beauchier, a man with forty years' experience of planting vines in the Lubéron. He personally pushed the small plough behind the tractor, making sure that lines were straight and correctly spaced, trudging up and down in his canvas boots, his leathery face rapt in concentration. The lines were staked at each end by bamboo rods and marked by lengths of twine. The field was now stripped and ready to be turned into a vineyard.

The new vines, about the size of my thumb and tipped with red wax, were unloaded from the vans while Monsieur Beauchier inspected his planting equipment. I had assumed that the planting would be done mechanically, but all I could see were a few hollow steel rods and a large triangle made of wood. The planting team gathered round and were assigned their duties, then jostled untidily into formation.

Beauchier led the way with the wooden triangle, which he used like a three-sided wheel, the points making equidistant marks in the earth. Two men followed him with steel rods, plunging them into the marks to make holes for the vines, which were planted and firmed in by the rearguard. The two women, Faustin's wife and daughter, dispensed vines, advice and fashion comments on the assortment of hats worn by the men, particularly Faustin's new and slightly rakish yachting cap. The dogs enjoyed themselves by getting in everyone's way, dodging kicks and tangling themselves in the twine.

As the day wore on, the planters became more widely spaced with Beauchier often two hundred yards in front of the stragglers at the back, but distance was no barrier to conversation. It appears to be part of the ritual that lengthy discussions are always conducted between the two people furthest away from each other, while the intervening members of the team curse the dogs and argue about the straightness of the lines. And so the raucous procession moved up and down the field until mid-afternoon, when Henriette produced two large baskets and work stopped for the Provençal version of a coffee break.

The team sat on a grassy bank above the vines, looking like a scene from Cartier-Bresson's scrapbook, and attacked the contents of the baskets. There were four litres of wine and an enormous pile of the sugared slices of fried bread called *tranches dorées*, dark gold in colour and crisp and delicious to taste. Grandfather André arrived to inspect what had been done, and we saw him poking the earth critically with his stick and then nodding his head. He came over for a glass of wine and sat in the sun, a benign old lizard, scratching a dog's stomach with the end of his muddy stick and asking Henriette what was for dinner. He wanted to eat early so that he could watch *Santa Barbara*, his favourite television soap opera.

The wine had all gone. The men stretched and brushed the crumbs from their mouths and went back to work. By late evening it was finished, and the ragged old melon field was now impeccable, the tiny dots of new vines just visible against the setting sun. The team gathered in our courtyard to unkink their backs and make inroads on the pastis, and I took Faustin to one side to ask him about payment. We'd had the tractor for three days, and dozens of hours of labour. What did we owe them? Faustin was so anxious to explain that he put down his glass. We would pay for the

vines, he said, but the rest was taken care of by the system which operated in the valley, with everyone contributing their time free when major replanting had to be done. It all evened out in the end, he said, and it avoided paperwork and tedious dealings with *les fiscs* about taxes. He smiled and tapped the side of his nose with a finger and then, as though it was a small matter hardly worth mentioning, he asked if we would like 250 asparagus plants put in while we still had the use of the tractor and the men. It was done the next day. So much for our theory that nothing happens fast in Provence.

* * * * *

The Lubéron sounded different in spring. Birds who had been ducking all winter came out of hiding now that the hunters were gone, and their song replaced gunfire. The only jarring noise I could hear as I walked along the path towards the Massot residence was a furious hammering, and I wondered if he had decided to put up a For Sale notice in preparation for the beginning of the tourist season.

I found him on the track beyond his house, contemplating a five-foot stake that he had planted at the edge of a clearing. A rusty piece of tin had been nailed to the top of the stake, with a single angry word daubed in white paint: *PRIVÉ!* Three more stakes and notices were lying on the track, together with a pile of boulders. Massot was obviously intending to barricade the clearing. He grunted good morning and picked up another stake, hammering it into the ground as if it had just insulted his mother.

I asked him what he was doing.

'Keeping out the Germans,' he said, and started to roll boulders into a rough cordon between the stakes.

The piece of land that he was sealing off was some distance from his house, and on the forest side of the track. It couldn't possibly belong to him, and I said I thought it was part of the national park.

'That's right,' he said, 'but I'm French. So it's more mine than the Germans.' He moved another boulder. 'Every summer they come here and put up their tents and make *merde* all over the forest.'

He straightened up and lit a cigarette, tossing the empty packet into the bushes. I asked him if he had thought that maybe one of the Germans might buy his house.

'Germans with tents don't buy anything except bread,' he said with a sniff of disdain. 'You should see their cars – stuffed with German sausage, German beer, tins of sauerkraut. They bring it all with them. Mean? They're real *pisse-vinaigres*.'

Massot, in his new role as protector of the countryside and authority on the economics of tourism, went on to explain the problem of the peasant in Provence. He admitted that tourists – even German tourists – brought money to the area, and that people who bought houses provided work for local builders. But look what they had done to property prices! It was a scandal. No farmer could afford to pay them. We tactfully avoided any discussion of Massot's own attempts at property speculation, and he sighed at the injustice of it all. Then he cheered up, and told me a house-buying story that had ended to his complete satisfaction.

There was a peasant who for years had coveted his neighbour's house; not for the house itself, which was almost a ruin, but for the land that was attached to it. He offered to buy the property, but his neighbour, taking advantage of the sharp rise in house prices, accepted a higher offer from a Parisian.

During the winter, the Parisian spent millions of francs renovating the house and installing a swimming pool. Finally, the work is finished, and the Parisian and his chic friends come down for the long First of May weekend. They are charmed by the house and amused by the quaint old peasant who lives next door, particularly by his habit of going to bed at 8 o'clock.

The Parisian household is awakened at four in the morning by Charlemagne, the peasant's large and noisy cockerel, who crows non-stop for two hours. The Parisian complains to the peasant. The peasant shrugs. It is the country. Cocks must crow. That is normal.

The next morning, and the morning after that, Charlemagne is up and crowing at four o'clock. Tempers are getting frayed, and the guests return to Paris early, to catch up on their sleep. The Parisian complains again to the peasant, and again the peasant shrugs. They part on hostile terms.

In August, the Parisian returns with a house full of guests. Charlemagne wakes them punctually every morning at four. Attempts at afternoon naps are foiled by the peasant, who is doing some work on his house with a jack-hammer and a loud concrete-mixer. The Parisian insists that the peasant silences his cockerel. The peasant refuses. After several heated exchanges, the Parisian takes the peasant to court, seeking an injunction to restrain Charlemagne. The verdict is in favour of the peasant, and the cockerel continues his early morning serenades.

Visits to the house eventually become so intolerable that the Parisian puts it up for sale. The peasant, acting through a friend, manages to buy most of the land.

The Sunday after the purchase goes through, the peasant and his friend celebrate with a huge lunch, the main course of which is Charlemagne, turned into a delicious *coq au vin*.

Massot thought that this was a fine story – defeat for the Parisian, victory and more land for the peasant, a good lunch – it had everything. I asked him if it was true, and he looked at me sideways, sucking on the ragged end of his moustache. 'It doesn't do to cross a peasant' was all he would say, and I thought that if I was a German camper I'd try Spain this summer.

* * * * *

Every day, as the weather stayed mild, there was fresh evidence of growth and greenery, and one of the most verdant patches of all was the swimming pool, which had turned a bilious emerald in the sunshine. It was time to call Bernard the *pisciniste* with his algae-fighting equipment before the plant life started crawling out of the deep end and through the front door.

A job like this is never done in Provence simply on the basis of a phone call and a verbal explanation. There has to be a preliminary visit of inspection – to walk around the problem, to nod know-ingly, to have a drink or two and then to make another rendezvous. It is a kind of limbering-up exercise, only to be skipped in cases of real emergency.

On the evening Bernard arrived to look at the pool, I was scrubbing at the garland of green fur that had developed just above the water line, and he watched me for a few moments before squatting down on his haunches and wagging a finger under my nose. Somehow I knew what his first word would be.

'*Non*,' he said, 'you mustn't scrub it. You must treat it. I will bring a product.' We abandoned the green fur and went indoors for a drink, and Bernard explained why he hadn't been able to come earlier. He had been suffering from toothache, but couldn't find a local dentist who was prepared to treat him, because of his strange affliction: he bites dentists. He can't stop himself. It is an incurable reflex. The moment he feels an exploratory finger in his mouth – *tak!* – he bites. He had so far bitten the only dentist in Bonnieux, and four dentists in Cavaillon, and had been obliged to go to Avignon, where he was unknown in dental circles. Fortunately, he had found a dentist who fought back with anaesthetic, knocking Bernard out completely while the repair work was done. The dentist told him afterwards that he had a mouthful of eighteenth-century teeth.

Eighteenth-century or not, they looked very white and healthy against Bernard's black beard as he laughed and talked. He was a man of great charm and, although born and raised in Provence, not at all a country bumpkin. He drank Scotch, the older the better, rather than pastis, and had married a girl from Paris whom we suspected of having a hand in the contents of his wardrobe. Not for him the canvas boots and the old blue trousers and frayed and faded shirts that we were used to seeing; Bernard was dapper, from his soft leather shoes to his large assortment of designer sunglasses. We wondered what kind of ensemble he would wear for the work of chlorinating and barnacle-scraping that was needed before the pool was ready for human occupation.

The day of the spring clean arrived, and Bernard bounded up the steps in sunglasses, grey flannels and blazer, twirling an umbrella in case the rain promised by the weather forecast should come our way. Following him with some difficulty was the secret of his continued elegance, a small, scruffy man weighed down with tubs of chlorine, brushes and a suction pump. This was Gaston, who was actually going to do the job under Bernard's supervision.

Later that morning, I went out to see how they were getting on.

A fine drizzle had set in, and the sodden Gaston was wrestling with the serpentine coils of the suction hose while Bernard, blazer slung nonchalantly round his shoulders, was directing operations from the shelter of his umbrella. There, I thought, is a man who understands how to delegate. If anyone could help us move our stone table into the courtyard, surely it was Bernard. I took him away from his duties at the poolside and we went to study the situation.

The table looked, bigger, heavier and more permanently settled in its garnish of weeds than ever, but Bernard was not discouraged. '*C'est pas méchant*,' he said, 'I know a man who could do it in half an hour.' I imagined a sweating giant heaving the great slabs around as a change from winning tug-of-war contests with teams of horses, but it was more prosaic than that. Bernard's man had just acquired a machine called *un bob*, a scaled-down version of a fork-lift truck, narrow enough to pass through the courtyard doorway. *Voilà*! It sounded easy.

The owner of *le bob* was telephoned and arrived within half an hour, eager to put his new machine into active service. He measured the width of the doorway and assessed the weight of the table. No problem; *bob* could do it. There was a small adjustment to be made here and there, but a mason could take care of that. It was merely a question of removing the lintel over the doorway – just for five minutes – to provide sufficient height for the load to pass through. I looked at the lintel. It was another piece of stone, four feet wide, nine inches thick and deeply embedded in the side of the house. It was major demolition, even to my inexpert eye. The table stayed where it was.

The wretched thing had become a daily frustration. Here we were with hot weather and the outdoor eating season just around the corner – the days we had dreamed about back in England and through the winter – and we had nowhere to put a bowl of olives, let alone a five-course lunch. We seriously considered calling Pierrot at the quarry and asking for an introduction to the Carcassonne rugby team, and then Providence arrived with a screech of brakes and a dusty cocker spaniel.

Didier had been working at a house on the other side of Saint-Rémy, and had been approached by a uniformed *gendarme*.

50

Would there be any interest, the *gendarme* wondered, in a load of weathered stone, the old, lichen-covered stuff, that could be used to give a new wall instant antiquity? It so happened that one of the jobs on Didier's long list was to build a wall at the front of our house, and he thought of us. The officer of the law wanted to be paid *au noir*, in cash, but stone like that was not easy to find. Would we like it?

We would happily have agreed to half a ton of bird droppings if it meant getting Didier and his entourage back; we had often thought of them as movers of the table before they disappeared, and this seemed like a wink from the gods. Yes, we would have the stone, and could he give us a hand with the table? He looked at it and grinned. 'Seven men,' he said. 'I'll come on Saturday with two when I bring the stone if you can find the rest.' We had a deal, and soon we would have a table. My wife started planning the first outdoor lunch of the year.

We lured three more or less able-bodied young men with the promise of food and drink, and when Didier and his assistants arrived the seven of us took up our positions round the table to go through the ritual of spitting on hands and deciding how best to negotiate the fifteen-yard journey. In circumstances like these, every Frenchman is an expert, and various theories were advanced: the table should be rolled on logs; no, it should be pulled on a wooden pallet; nonsense, it could be pushed most of the way by truck. Didier let everyone finish, and then ordered us to pick it up, two to each side, with him taking one side on his own.

With a reluctant squelch, the slab came out of the ground, and we staggered the first five yards, veins popping with effort while Didier kept up a running commentary of directions. Another five yards, and then we had to stop to turn it so that it could get through the doorway. The weight was brutal, and we were already sweating and aching, and at least one of us thought that he was getting a little old for this kind of work, but the table was now on its side and ready to be inched into the courtyard.

'This,' said Didier, 'is the amusing part.' There was only enough room for two men either side of the slab, and they would have to take the weight while the others pushed and pulled. Two enormous webbing straps were passed under the table, there was more spitting on hands, and my wife disappeared into the house, unable to watch the mashing of feet and four men having simultaneous ruptures. 'Whatever you do,' said Didier, 'don't drop it. *Allez!*' And with curses and skinned knuckles and a chorus of grunts that would have done credit to an elephant in labour, the table slowly crossed the threshold and at long last entered the courtyard.

We compared wounds and sprains before setting up the base – a relatively insignificant structure weighing no more than 300 pounds – and coating its top with cement. One final heave, and the slab went on, but Didier wasn't satisfied; it was a hair's-breadth off centre. Eric the chief assistant was required to kneel under the table on all fours. He supported most of the weight on his back while the top was centred, and I wondered if my insurance covered death on the premises by crushing. To my relief, Eric surfaced without any visible injury, although, as Didier said cheerfully, it's the internal damage that slows a man down in his line of work. I hoped he was joking.

Beers were passed round, and the table was admired. It looked just as we'd imagined on that afternoon in February when we had traced the outline in the snow. It was a good size, and handsome against the stone of the courtyard wall. The perspiration stains and smudges of blood would soon dry off, and then lunch could be served.

In our anticipation of all the pleasures of long outdoor meals there was only one slight regret, because we were coming to the very end of the season for that ugly but delicious fungus which is almost worth its weight in gold, the fresh Vaucluse truffle.

The truffle world is secretive, but strangers can get a glimpse of it by going to one of the villages round Carpentras. There, the cafés do a brisk trade in breakfast jolts of *marc* and Calvados, and an unknown face coming through the door brings muttered conversations to a sudden stop. Outside, men stand in tight, preoccupied groups looking, sniffing and finally weighing wart-encrusted, earth-covered lumps that are handled with reverential care. Money passes, fat, grimy wads of it, in 100, 200 and 500 franc notes, which are double-checked with much licking of thumbs. Attention from outsiders is not welcomed.

This informal market is an early stage in the process which leads to the tables of three-star restaurants and the counters of ruinously expensive Parisian delicatessens like Fauchon and Hédiard. But even here in the middle of nowhere, buying direct from men with dirt under their fingernails and yesterday's garlic on their breath, with dented, wheezing cars, with old baskets or plastic bags instead of smart attaché cases – even here, the prices are, as they like to say, *très sérieux*. Truffles are sold by weight, and the standard unit is the kilo. At 1987 prices, a kilo of truffles bought in the village market cost at least 2,000 francs, payable in cash. Cheques are not accepted, receipts are never given, because the *truffiste* is not anxious to participate in the crackpot government scheme the rest of us call income tax.

So the starting price is 2,000 francs a kilo. With a little massaging along the way from various agents and middlemen, by the time the truffle reaches its spiritual home in the kitchens of Bocuse or Troisgros the price will probably have doubled. At Fauchon, it could easily have reached 5,000 francs a kilo, but at least they accept cheques.

There are two reasons why these absurd prices continue to be paid, and continue to rise – the first, obviously, being that nothing in the world smells or tastes like fresh truffles except fresh truffles. The second is that, despite all the effort and ingenuity that the French have brought to bear on the problem, they haven't been able to cultivate the truffle. They continue to try, and it is not uncommon in the Vaucluse to come across fields that have been planted with truffle-oaks and keep-off notices. But the propagation of truffles seems to be a haphazard affair which is only understood by nature – thus adding to the rarity and the price – and human attempts at truffle breeding haven't come to much. Until they do, there is only one way to enjoy truffles without spending a small fortune, and that is to find them yourself.

We were lucky enough to be given a free course in truffle-hunting techniques by our almost resident expert, Ramon the plasterer. He had tried everything over the years, and admitted to some modest success. He was generous with his advice and, as he smoothed on his plaster and drank his beer, he told us exactly what to do. (He didn't tell us where to go, but then no truffle man would.)

It all depends, he said, on timing, knowledge and patience, and the possession of a pig, a trained hound or a stick. Truffles grow a few centimetres under the ground, on the roots of certain oak or hazel-nut trees. During the season, from November until March, they can be tracked down by nose, providing you have sensitive enough equipment. The supreme truffle detector is the pig, who is born with a fondness for the taste, and whose sense of smell in this case is superior to the dog's. But there is a snag: the pig is not content to wag his tail and point when he has discovered a truffle. He wants to eat it. In fact, he is desperate to eat it. And, as Ramon said, you cannot reason with a pig on the brink of gastronomic ecstasy. He is not easily distracted, nor is he of a size you can fend off with one hand while you rescue the truffle with the other. There he is, as big as a small tractor, rigid with porcine determination and refusing to be budged. Given this fundamental design fault, we weren't surprised when Ramon told us that the lighter and more amenable dog had become increasingly popular.

Unlike pigs, dogs do not instinctively rootle for truffles; they have to be trained, and Ramon favoured the *saucisson* method. You take a slice and rub it with a truffle, or dip it in truffle juice, so that the dog begins to associate the smell of truffles with a taste of heaven. Little by little, or by leaps and bounds if the dog is both intelligent and a gourmet, he will come to share your enthusiasm for truffles, and he will be ready for field trials. If your training has been thorough, if your dog is temperamentally suited to the work, and if you know where to go, you might find yourself with a *chien truffier* who will point the way to the buried treasure. Then, just as he begins to dig for it, you bribe him away with a slice of treated sausage and uncover what you hope will be a lump of black gold.

Ramon himself had eventually settled on another method, the stick technique, which he demonstrated for us, tiptoeing across the kitchen with an imaginary wand held in front of him. Once again, you have to know where to go, but this time you have to wait for the right weather conditions as well. When the sun is shining on the roots of a likely-looking oak, approach cautiously and, with your stick, prod gently around the base of the tree. If a startled fly should rise vertically from the vegetation, mark the spot and dig.

You might have disturbed a member of the fly family whose genetic passion is to lay its eggs on the truffle (doubtless adding a certain *je ne sais quoi* to the flavour). Many peasants in the Vaucluse had adopted this technique because walking around with a stick is less conspicuous than walking around with a pig, and secrecy can be more easily preserved. Truffle hunters like to protect their sources.

The finding of truffles, chancy and unpredictable though it is, began to seem almost straightforward when compared with the skulduggery that goes on in the sales and distribution department. With the relish of an investigative reporter, and frequent winks and nudges, Ramon took us through the most common of the murky practices.

With everything edible in France, certain areas have the reputation for producing the best – the best olives from Nyons, the best mustard from Dijon, the best melons from Cavaillon, the best cream from Normandy. The best truffles, it is generally agreed, come from the Périgord, and naturally one pays more for them. But how do you know that the truffle you buy in Cahors hasn't been dug up several hundred kilometres away in the Vaucluse? Unless you know and trust your supplier, you can't be sure, and Ramon's inside information was that 50 per cent of the truffles sold in the Périgord were born elsewhere and 'naturalised'.

Then there is the uncanny business of the truffle which somehow gains weight between leaving the ground and arriving on the scales. It could be that it has been gift-wrapped in an extra coating of earth. On the other hand, it could be that a heavier substance altogether has found its way inside the truffle itself – invisible until, in mid-slice, your knife lays bare a sliver of metal. *Ils sont vilains, ces types!* Even if you are prepared to sacrifice the flavour of fresh truffles for the protection offered by the canned variety – even then, you can't be sure. One hears rumours. It has been hinted that some French cans with French labels actually contain Italian or Spanish truffles. (Which, if true, must be one of the most profitable and least publicised acts of co-operation ever between Common Market countries.)

Yet, for all the whispers of chicanery and prices which become more ridiculous each year, the French continue to follow their noses and dig into their pockets, and we found ourselves doing the same when we heard that the last truffles of the season were being served at one of our favourite local restaurants.

Chez Michel is the village bar of Cabrières and the headquarters of the *boules* club, and not sufficiently upholstered or pompous to attract too much attention from the Guide Michelin inspectors. Old men play cards in the front; clients of the restaurant eat very well in the back. The owner cooks, Madame his wife takes the orders, members of the family help at table and in the kitchens. It is a comfortable neighbourhood *bistrot* with no apparent intention of joining the culinary merry-go-round which turns talented cooks into brand names and pleasant restaurants into temples of the expense account.

Madame sat us down and gave us a drink, and we asked how the truffles were. She rolled her eyes and an expression close to pain crossed her face. For a moment we thought they had all gone, but it was simply her reaction to one of life's many unfairnesses, which she then explained to us.

Her husband Michel loves to cook with fresh truffles. He has his suppliers, and he pays, as everyone must, in cash, without the benefit of a receipt. For him, this is a substantial and legitimate business cost which cannot be set against the profits because there is no supporting evidence on paper to account for the outlay. Also, he refuses to raise the price of his menus, even when they are studded with truffles, to a level which might offend his regular customers. (In winter, the clientele is local, and careful with its money; the big spenders don't usually come down until Easter.)

This was the problem, and Madame was doing her best to be philosophical about it as she showed us a copper pan containing several thousand francs' worth of non-deductible truffles. We asked her why Michel did it, and she gave a classic shrug – shoulders and eyebrows going upwards in unison, corners of the mouth turning down. *'Pour faire plaisir,'* she said.

We had omelettes. They were moist and fat and fluffy, with a tiny deep black nugget of truffle in every mouthful, a last rich taste of winter. We wiped our plates with bread and tried to guess what a treat like this would cost in London, and came to the conclusion that we had just eaten a bargain. Comparison with London is a sure way of justifying any minor extravagance in Provence.

Michel came out of the kitchen to make his rounds and noticed our bone-clean plates. 'They were good, the truffles?' Better than good, we said. He told us that the dealer who had sold them to him – one of the old rogues in the business – had just been robbed. The thief had taken a cardboard box stuffed with cash, more than 100,000 francs, but the dealer hadn't dared to report the loss for fear that embarrassing questions might be asked about where the money had come from. Now he was pleading poverty. Next year his prices would be higher. *C'est la vie.*

We got home to find the telephone ringing. It is a sound which both of us detest, and there is always a certain amount of manoeuvring to see who can avoid answering it. We have an innate pessimism about telephone calls; they have a habit of coming at the wrong time, and they are too sudden, catapulting you into a conversation you weren't expecting. Letters, on the other hand, are a pleasure to receive, not least because they allow you to consider your reply. But people don't write letters any more. They're too busy, they're in too much of a hurry or, dismissing the service which manages to deliver bills with unfailing reliability, they don't trust the post. We were learning not to trust the telephone, and I picked it up as I would a long-dead fish.

'How's the weather?' asked an unidentified voice.

I said that the weather was good. It must have made all the difference, because the caller then introduced himself as Tony. He wasn't a friend, or even a friend of a friend, but an acquaintance of an acquaintance. 'Looking for a house down there,' he said, in the clipped, time-is-money voice that executives adopt when they talk on their car phones to their wives. 'Thought you could give me a hand. Want to get in before the Easter rush and the frogs put up the prices.'

I offered to give him the names of some property agents. 'Bit of a problem there,' he said. 'Don't speak the language. Order a meal, of course, but that's about it.' I offered to give him the name of a bi-lingual agent, but that wouldn't do. 'Don't want to get tied up with one firm. Bad move. No leverage.'

We had reached the moment in the conversation when I was

supposed to offer my services, or else say something to terminate this budding relationship before it could bud any further, but the chance was denied me.

'Must go. Can't chat all night. Plenty of time for that when I get down next week.' And then those awful words which put an end to any hopes of hiding: 'Don't worry. I've got your address. I'll find you.'

The line went dead.

* * * * *

APRIL

It was one of those mornings when the early mist hung in wet sheets along the valley under a band of bright blue sky and, by the time we came home from walking, the dogs were sleek with damp, whiskers glittering in the sun. They saw the stranger first, and pranced round him pretending to be fierce.

He stood by the swimming pool, fending off their attentions with a handbag of masculine design and backing ever closer to the deep end. He seemed relieved to see us.

'Dogs all right, are they? Not rabid or anything?' The voice was recognisable as that of our telephone caller, Tony from London, and he and his handbag joined us for breakfast. He was large and prosperously padded round the waistline, with tinted glasses, carefully tousled hair and the pale-coloured casual clothes that English visitors wear in Provence regardless of the weather. He sat down and produced from his bag a bulging Filofax, a gold pen, a packet of duty-free Cartier cigarettes and a gold lighter. His watch was also gold. I was sure that gold medallions nestled in his chest hair. He told us he was in advertising.

He gave us a brief but extremely complimentary account of his business history. He had started his own advertising agency, built it up – 'tough business, bloody competitive' – and had just sold a controlling interest for what he described as heavy money and a five-year contract. Now, he said, he was able to relax, although one would never have guessed from his behaviour that he was a man who had left the cares of office behind. He was in a constant fidget, looking at his watch, arranging and re-arranging his trinkets on the table in front of him, adjusting his glasses and smoking in deep, distracted drags. Suddenly, he stood up.

'Mind if I make a quick call? What's the code for London?'

My wife and I had come to expect this as an inevitable part of welcoming the Englishman abroad into our home. He comes in, he has a drink or a cup of coffee, he makes a 'phone call to check that his business has not collapsed during the first few hours of his absence. The routine never varies, and the substance of the call is as predictable as the routine.

'Hi, it's me. Yes, I'm calling from Provence. Everything OK? Any messages? Oh. None? David didn't call back? Oh shit. Look, I'll be moving around a bit today, but you can reach me on (what's the number here?) Got that? What? Yes, the weather's fine. Call you later.'

Tony put the 'phone down and reassured us about the state of his company, which was managing to stumble along without him. He was now ready to devote his energies, and ours, to the purchase of property.

Buying a house in Provence is not without its complications, and it is easy to understand why busy and efficient people from cities, used to firm decisions and quickly-struck deals, often give up after months of serpentine negotiations that have led nowhere. The first of many surprises, always greeted with alarm and disbelief, is that all property costs more than its advertised price. Most of this is because the French government takes a cut of about eight per cent on all transactions. Then there are the legal fees, which are high. And it is sometimes a condition of the sale that the purchaser pays the agent's commission of three to five per cent. An unlucky buyer could end up paying as much as fifteen per cent on top of the price.

There is, however, a well-established ritual of respectable cheating which has the double attractions, so dear to every French heart, of saving money and screwing the government. This is the two-price purchase, and a typical example would work as follows: Monsieur Rivarel, a businessman in Aix, wishes to sell an old country house that he inherited. He wants a million francs. As it is not his principal residence, he will be liable for tax on the proceeds of the sale, a thought which causes him great distress. He therefore decides that the official, recorded price – the *prix déclaré* – will be 600,000 francs, and he will grit his teeth and pay tax on that. His consolation is that the balance of 400,000 francs will be paid in cash, under the table. This, as he will point out, is an *affaire intéressante* not only for him, but for the buyer, because the official fees and charges will be based on the lower, declared price. Voilà! Everyone is happy.

The practical aspects of this arrangement call for a sense of timing and great delicacy on the part of the lawyer, or *notaire*, when the moment comes to sign the act of sale. All the interested parties – the buyer, the seller and the property agent – are gathered in the *notaire*'s office, and the act of sale is read aloud, line by interminable line. The price marked on the contract is 600,000 francs. The 400,000 in cash which the buyer has brought along has to be passed to the seller, but it would be highly improper if this were to happen in front of the *notaire*. Consequently, he feels a pressing need to go to the lavatory, where he stays until the cash has been counted and has changed hands. He can then return, accept the cheque for the declared price, and supervise the signing ceremony without having compromised his legal reputation. It has been said, rather unkindly, that two basic requirements for a rural *notaire* are a blind eye and a diplomatic bladder.

But there can be many obstacles to overcome before the visit to the *notaire*, and one of the most common is the problem of multiple ownership. Under French law, property is normally inherited by the children, with each child having an equal share. All of them must be in agreement before their inheritance is sold, and the more children there are the less likely this becomes, as is the case with an old farmhouse not far from us. It has been passed down from one generation to the next, and ownership is now divided between fourteen cousins, three of whom are of Corsican extraction and thus, according to our French friends, impossible to deal with. Prospective buyers have made their offers, but at any given time nine cousins might accept, two would be undecided, and the Corsicans would say no. The farm remains unsold, and will doubtless pass to the thirty-eight children of the fourteen cousins. Eventually, it will be owned by 175 distant relatives who don't trust each other.

Even if the property should be owned outright by a single acquisitive peasant, such as Massot, there is no guarantee of a straightforward transaction. The peasant may set a price which he thinks is absurdly high, and which will keep him in drink and lottery tickets for the rest of his days. A buyer comes along and agrees the inflated price. The peasant immediately suspects trickery. It's too easy. The price must be too low. He withdraws the house from the market for six months before trying again at a higher figure.

And then there are the trifling inconveniences that are mentioned casually at the last minute: an outbuilding that has been lost to a neighbour in a card game; an ancient right of way which technically permits the passage of herds of goats through the kitchen twice a year; a dispute over well water that has been bitter and unresolved since 1958; the venerable sitting tenant who is bound to die before next spring – there is always something unexpected, and a buyer needs patience and a sense of humour to see the business through.

I tried to prepare Tony for these local oddities as we drove to the office of a property agent whom we knew, but I should have saved my breath. He was, by his own modest admission, a shrewd and resourceful negotiator. He had played hardball with the big boys on Madison Avenue, and it would take more than bureaucracy or a French peasant to get the better of him. I began to doubt the wisdom of introducing him to anyone who didn't have a car 'phone and a personal business manager.

The agent met us at the door of her office, and sat us down with two thick files of property details and photographs. She spoke no English and Tony spoke vestigial French, and since direct communication was impossible he behaved as if she wasn't there. It was a particularly arrogant form of bad manners, made worse by the assumption that even the most derogatory language can be used without the risk of it being understood. And so I passed an embarrassing half hour as Tony flicked through the files, muttering 'Fuck me!' and 'They must be joking' at intervals while I made feeble attempts to translate his comments into some nonsense about his being impressed by the prices.

He had started with the firm intention of finding a village house with no land. He was far too busy to bother with a garden. But as he went through the properties I could see him mentally becoming the Provençal squire with acres of vines and olives. By the time he had finished he was worrying about where he should put his tennis court. To my disappointment, there were three properties which he thought worthy of his attention.

'We'll do those this afternoon,' he announced, making notes in his Filofax and looking at his watch. I thought he was going to commandeer the agent's 'phone for an international call, but he was just reacting to a signal from his stomach. 'Let's hit a restaurant,' he said, 'and we can be back here by two.' The agent smiled and nodded as Tony waved two fingers at her and we left the poor woman to recover.

At lunch, I told Tony that I wouldn't be going with him and the agent that afternoon. He was surprised that I had anything better to do, but ordered a second bottle of wine and told me that money was an international language and he didn't anticipate having any difficulties. Unfortunately, when the bill arrived he discovered that neither his gold American Express card nor the wad of traveller's cheques that he hadn't had time to change were of any interest to the restaurant's proprietor. I paid, and made some remark about the international language. Tony was not amused.

I left him with mixed feelings of relief and guilt. Boors are always unpleasant, but when you're in a foreign country and they are of your own nationality you feel some kind of vague responsibility. The next day, I called the agent to apologise. 'Don't worry,' she said, 'Parisians are often just as bad. At least I couldn't understand what he was saying.'

* * * * *

A final confirmation that warmer weather was here to stay was provided by Monsieur Menicucci's wardrobe. He had come to carry out the preliminary *études* for his summer project, which was our central heating. His woollen bonnet had been replaced by a lightweight cotton model decorated with a slogan advertising sanitary fittings, and instead of his thermal snow shoes he was wearing brown canvas bootees. His assistant, *jeune*, was in a guerilla outfit of army fatigues and jungle cap, and the two of them marched through the house taking measurements as Menicucci delivered himself of assorted *pensées*.

Music was his first subject today. He and his wife had just attended an official artisans and plumbers lunch, followed by ballroom dancing, which was one of his many accomplishments. 'Yes, Monsieur Peter,' he said, 'we danced until six. I had the feet of a young man of eighteen.' I could picture him, nimble and exact, whirling Madame around the floor, and I wondered if he had a special ballroom bonnet for these occasions, because it was impossible to think of him bareheaded. I must have smiled at the thought. 'I know,' he said, 'you're thinking that the waltz is not serious music. For that one must listen to the great composers.'

He then expounded a remarkable theory, which had occurred to him while he was playing the clarinet during one of the power cuts that the French electricity board arranges at regular intervals. Electricity, he said, is a matter of science and logic. Classical music is a matter of art and logic. *Vous voyez?* Already one sees a common factor. And when you listen to the disciplined and logical progression of some of Mozart's work, the conclusion is inescapable: Mozart would have made a formidable electrician.

I was saved from replying by *jeune*, who had finished counting up the number of radiators we would need, and had arrived at a figure of twenty. Menicucci received the news with a wince, shaking his hand as if he'd burned his fingers. '*Oh là là*. This will cost more than *centimes*.' He mentioned several million francs, saw my shocked expression and then divided by a hundred; he had been quoting in old money. Even so, it was a considerable amount. There was the high cost of cast iron, plus the government sales tax, or TVA, of 18·6 per cent. This led him to mention an outrageous fiscal irregularity which typified the villainy of politicians.

'You buy a bidet,' he said, jabbing me with his finger, 'and you pay full TVA. The same for a washer or a screw. But I will tell you something *scandaleux* and altogether wrong. You buy a pot of caviar, and you will pay only 6 per cent TVA, because it is classified as *nourriture*. Now tell me this: who eats caviar?' I pleaded not guilty. 'I will tell you. It is the politicians, the millionaires, the *grosses légumes* in Paris – they are the ones who eat caviar. It's an outrage.' He stumped off, fulminating about caviar orgies in the Elysée Palace, to check *jeune*'s radiator arithmetic.

The thought of Menicucci occupying the premises for five or six weeks, burrowing his way through the thick old walls with a drill that was almost as big as he was and filling the air with dust and running commentaries was not a treat to look forward to. It would be a dirty and tedious process involving almost every room in the house. But one of the joys of Provence, we told ourselves, was that we could live outdoors while this was going on. Even this early in the year, the days were very nearly hot, and we decided to start the outdoor season in earnest one Sunday morning when the sun coming through the bedroom window woke us up at seven o'clock.

All good Sundays include a trip to the market, and we were in Coustellet by eight. The space behind the disused station was lined with elderly trucks and vans, each with a trestle table set up in front. A blackboard showed the day's prices for vegetables. The stallholders, already tanned from the fields, were eating croissants and brioches that were still warm from the bakery across the street. We watched as one old man sliced a baguette lengthways with a wooden-handled pocket knife and spread on fresh goat's cheese in a creamy layer before pouring himself a glass of red wine from the litre bottle that would keep him going until lunchtime.

The Coustellet market is small, compared to the weekly markets in Cavaillon and Apt and Isle-sur-la-Sorgue, and not yet fashionable. Customers carry baskets instead of cameras, and only in July and August are you likely to see the occasional haughty woman down from Paris with her Dior track suit and small, nervous dog.

For the rest of the season, from spring until autumn, it is just the local inhabitants, and the peasants who bring in what they have taken from the earth or the greenhouse a few hours earlier.

We walked slowly along the rows of trestle tables, admiring the merciless French housewife at work. Unlike us, she is not content merely to look at the produce before buying. She gets to grips with it – squeezing aubergines, sniffing tomatoes, snapping the match-stick-thin *haricots verts* between her fingers, poking suspiciously into the damp green hearts of lettuces, tasting cheeses and olives – and, if they don't come up to her private standards, she will glare at the stallholder as if she has been betrayed before taking her custom elsewhere.

At one end of the market, a van from the wine co-operative was surrounded by men rinsing their teeth thoughtfully in the new rosé. Next to them, a woman was selling free-range eggs and live rabbits, and beyond her the tables were piled high with vegetables, small and fragrant bushes of basil, tubs of lavender honey, great green bottles of first pressing olive oil, trays of hothouse peaches, pots of black *tapenade*, flowers and herbs, jams and cheeses – everything looked delicious in the early morning sun.

We bought red peppers to roast and big brown eggs and basil and peaches and goat's cheese and lettuce and pink-streaked onions. And, when the basket could hold no more, we went across the road to buy half a yard of bread – the *gros pain* that makes such a tasty mop for any olive oil or vinaigrette sauce that is left on the plate. The bakery was crowded and noisy, and smelt of warm dough and the almonds that had gone into the morning's cakes. While we waited, we remembered being told that the French spend as much of their income on their stomachs as the English do on their cars and stereo systems, and we could easily believe it.

Everyone seemed to be shopping for a regiment. One round, jolly woman bought six large loaves – three yards of bread – a chocolate brioche the size of a hat, and an entire wheel of apple tart, the thin slices of apple packed in concentric rings, shining under a glaze of apricot sauce. We were aware that we had missed breakfast.

Lunch made up for it: cold roasted peppers, slippery with olive oil and speckled with fresh basil, tiny mussels wrapped in bacon

and barbecued on skewers, salad and cheese. The sun was hot and the wine had made us sleepy. And then we heard the 'phone.

It is a rule of life that, when the 'phone rings between noon and three on a Sunday, the caller is English; a Frenchman wouldn't dream of interrupting the most relaxed meal of the week. I should have let it ring. Tony from advertising was back, and judging by the absence of static on the line he was hideously close.

'Just thought I'd touch base with you.' I could hear him taking a drag on his cigarette, and I made a mental note to buy an answering machine to deal with anyone else who might want to touch base on a Sunday.

'I think I've found a place.' He didn't pause to hear the effect of his announcement, and so missed the sound of my heart sinking. 'Quite a way from you, actually, nearer the coast.' I told him that I was delighted; the nearer the coast he was, the better. 'Needs a lot doing to it, so I'm not going to pay what he's asking. Thought I'd bring my builders over to do the work. They did the office in six weeks, top to bottom. Irish, but bloody good. They could sort this place out in a month.'

I was tempted to encourage him, because the idea of a gang of Irish workmen exposed to the pleasures of a building site in Provence – the sun, cheap wine, endless possibilities for delay and a proprietor too far away to be a daily nuisance – had the makings of a fine comic interlude, and I could see Mr. Murphy and his team stretching the job out until October, maybe getting the family over from Donegal for a holiday during August and generally having a grand time. I told Tony he might be better advised to hire local labour, and to get an architect to hire it for him.

'Don't need an architect,' he said, 'I know exactly what I want.' He would. 'Why should I pay him an arm and a leg for a couple of drawings?' There was no helping him. He knew best. I asked him when he was going back to England. 'This evening,' he said, and then guided me through the next hectic pages of his Filofax: a client meeting on Monday, three days in New York, a sales conference in Milton Keynes. He reeled it off with the mock weariness of the indispensable executive, and he was welcome to every second of it. 'Anyway,' he said, 'I'll keep in touch. I won't finalise on the house for a week or two, but I'll let you know as soon as I've inked it.'

My wife and I sat by the pool and wondered, not for the first time, why we both found it so difficult to get rid of thick-skinned and ungracious people. More of them would be coming down during the summer, baying for food and drink and a bedroom, for days of swimming and lifts to the airport. We didn't think of ourselves as anti-social or reclusive, but our brief experience with the thrustful and dynamic Tony had been enough to remind us that the next few months would require firmness and ingenuity. And an answering machine.

The approach of summer had obviously been on Massot's mind as well, because when I saw him a few days later in the forest he was busy adding a further refinement to his anti-camper defences. Under the signs he had nailed up saying *PRIVÉ!* he was fixing a second series of unwelcoming messages, short but sinister: *Attention! Vipères!* It was the perfect deterrent – full of menace, but without the need for visible proof that is the great drawback of other discouragements such as guard dogs, electrified fences and patrols armed with sub-machine guns. Even the most resolute camper would think twice before tucking himself up in a sleeping bag which might have one of the local residents coiled at the bottom. I asked Massot if there really were vipers in the Lubéron, and he shook his head at yet another example of the ignorance of foreigners.

'*Eh oui*,' he said, 'not big' – he held his hands up, about twelve inches apart – 'but if you're bitten you need to get to a doctor within forty-five minutes, or else . . .' He pulled a dreadful face, head to one side, tongue lolling from the side of his mouth, 'They say that when a viper bites a man, the man dies. But when a viper bites a woman' – he leaned forward and waggled his eyebrows – 'the viper dies.' He snorted with amusement and offered me one of his fat yellow cigarettes. 'Don't ever go walking without a good pair of boots.'

The Lubéron viper, according to Professor Massot, will normally avoid humans, and will attack only if provoked. When this happens, Massot's advice was to run in zig-zags, and preferably uphill, because an enraged viper can sprint – in short, straight bursts on level ground – as fast as a running man. I looked nervously around me, and Massot laughed. 'Of course, you can always try the peasant's trick: catch it behind the head and squeeze until its mouth is wide open. Spit hard into the mouth and *plok*! – he's dead.' He spat in demonstration, hitting one of the dogs on the head. 'But best of all,' said Massot, 'is to take a woman with you. They can't run as fast as men, and the viper will catch them first.' He went home to his breakfast leaving me to pick my way cautiously through the forest and practise my spitting.

* * * * *

Easter weekend arrived, and our cherry trees – about thirty of them – blossomed in unison. From the road, the house looked as if it were floating on a pink and white sea, and motorists were stopping to take photographs or walking tentatively up the drive until barking from the dogs turned them back. One group, more adventurous than the rest, drove up to the house in a car with Swiss plates and parked on the verge. I went to see what they wanted.

'We will picnic here,' the driver told me.

'I'm sorry, it's a private house.'

'No, no,' he said, waving a map at me, 'this is the Lubéron.'

'No, no,' I said, 'that's the Lubéron,' and pointed to the mountains.

'But I can't take my car up *there*.'

Eventually he drove off, puffing with Swiss indignation and leaving deep wheel marks in the grass we were trying to turn into a lawn. The tourist season had begun.

Up in the village on Easter Sunday, the small parking area was full, and not one of the cars had local plates. The visitors explored the narrow streets, looking curiously into people's houses and posing for photographs in front of the church. The young man who spends all day sitting on a doorstep next to the *épicerie* was asking everyone who passed for ten francs to make a 'phone call and taking the proceeds into the café.

The Café du Progrès has made a consistent and successful effort to avoid being picturesque. It is an interior decorator's nightmare, with tables and chairs that wobble and don't match, gloomy paintwork and a lavatory that splutters and gurgles often and noisily next to a shabby ice cream cabinet. The proprietor is gruff, and his dogs are indescribably matted. There is, however, a long and spectacular view from the glassed-in terrace next to the lavatory, and it's a good place to have a beer and watch the play of light on the hills and villages that stretch away towards the Basses-Alpes. A hand-lettered notice warns you not to throw cigarette ends out of the window, following complaints from the clientele of the open-air restaurant below, but if you observe this rule you will be left undisturbed. The regulars stay at the bar; the *terrasse* is for tourists, and on Easter Sunday it was crowded.

There were the Dutch, wholesome in their hiking boots and backpacks; the Germans, armed with Leicas and heavy costume jewellery; the Parisians, disdainful and smart, inspecting their glasses carefully for germs; an Englishman in sandals and an open-necked striped business shirt, working out his holiday finances on a pocket calculator while his wife wrote postcards to neighbours in Surrey. The dogs nosed among the tables looking for sugar lumps, causing the hygiene-conscious Parisians to shrink away. An Yves Montand song on the radio fought a losing battle with the sanitary sound effects, and empty pastis glasses were banged on the bar as the locals started to drift off towards home and lunch.

Outside the café, three cars had converged and were growling at each other. If one of them had reversed ten yards, they could all have passed, but a French driver considers it a moral defeat to give way, just as he feels a moral obligation to park wherever he can cause maximum inconvenience and to overtake on a blind bend. They say that Italians are dangerous drivers, but for truly lethal insanity I would back a Frenchman hurtling down the N100, late and hungry, against all comers.

I drove back from the village and just missed the first accident of the season. An old white Peugeot had gone backwards into a wooden telegraph pole at the bottom of the drive with sufficient force to snap the pole in two. There was no other car to be seen, and the road was dry and dead straight. It was difficult to work out how the back of the car and the pole had contrived to meet with such force. A young man was standing in the middle of the road, scratching his head. He grinned as I pulled up.

I asked him if he was hurt. 'I'm fine,' he said, 'but I think the car is *foutu.*' I looked at the telegraph pole, which was bent over the car, kept from falling by the sagging 'phone line. That also was *foutu*.

'We must hurry,' said the young man. 'Nobody must know.' He put a finger to his lips. 'Can you give me a lift home? It's just up the road. I need the tractor.' He got into the car, and the cause of the accident became clear; he smelt as though he had been marinated in Ricard. He explained that the car had to be removed with speed and secrecy. If the Post Office found that he had attacked one of their poles they would make him pay for it. 'Nobody must know,' he repeated, and hiccupped once or twice for emphasis.

I dropped him off and went home. Half an hour later, I went out to see if the stealthy removal of the car had been accomplished, but it was still there. So was a group of peasants, arguing noisily. Also two other cars and a tractor, which was blocking the road. As I watched, another car arrived and the driver sounded his horn to get the tractor to move. The man on the tractor pointed at the wreck and shrugged. The horn sounded again, this time in a continuous blare that bounced off the mountains and must have been audible in Ménerbes, two kilometres away.

The commotion lasted for another half hour before the Peugeot was finally extracted from the ditch and the secret motorcade disappeared in the direction of the local garage, leaving the telegraph pole creaking ominously in the breeze. The Post Office men came to replace it the following week, and attracted a small crowd. They asked one of the peasants what had happened. He shrugged innocently. 'Who knows?' he said. 'Woodworm?'

* * * * *

Our friend from Paris examined his empty glass with surprise, as if evaporation had taken place while he wasn't looking. I poured some more wine and he settled back in his chair, face tilted up to the sun.

'We still have the heating on in Paris,' he said, and took a sip of the cool, sweet wine from Beaumes de Venise. 'And it's been raining for weeks. I can see why you like it here. Mind you, it wouldn't suit me.'

It seemed to be suiting him well enough, basking in the warmth after a good lunch, but I didn't argue with him.

'You'd hate it,' I said. 'You'd probably get skin cancer from the sun and cirrhosis of the liver from too much plonk, and if you were ever feeling well enough you'd miss the theatre. And anyway, what would you do all day?'

He squinted at me drowsily, and put his sunglasses on. 'Exactly.'

It was part of what had become a familiar litany:

Don't you miss your friends?

No. They come and see us here.

Don't you miss English television?

No.

There must be *something* about England you miss?

Marmalade.

And then would come the real question, delivered half-humorously, half-seriously: what do you *do* all day? Our friend from Paris put it another way.

'Don't you get bored?'

We didn't. We never had time. We found the everyday curiosities of French rural life amusing and interesting. We were enjoying the gradual process of changing the house around so that it suited the way we lived. There was the garden to be designed and planted, a *boules* court to be built, a new language to be learned, villages and vineyards and markets to be discovered – the days went quickly enough without any other distractions, and there were always plenty of those. The previous week, as it happened, had been particularly rich in interruptions.

They started on Monday with a visit from Marcel the Parcel, our postman. He was irritated, barely pausing to shake hands before demanding to know where I had hidden the mail box. He had his rounds to do, it was almost noon, how could I expect him to deliver letters if he had to play *cache-cache* with the mail box? But we hadn't hidden it. So far as I knew, it was down at the end of the drive, firmly planted on a steel post. '*Non*,' said the postman, 'it has been moved.' There was nothing for it but to walk down the drive together and spend a fruitless five minutes searching the bushes to see if it had been knocked over. There was no sign that a mail box had ever been there except a small post hole in the ground. '*Voilà*,' said the postman, 'it is as I told you.' I found it hard to believe that anyone would steal a mail box, but he knew better. 'It is quite normal,' he said, 'people round here are *mal fini*.' I asked him what that meant. 'Mad.'

Back to the house we went, to restore his good humour with a drink and to discuss the installation of a new mail box that he would be happy to sell me. We agreed that it should be built into the side of an old well, positioned at the regulation height of 70 centimetres above the ground so that he could drop letters in without having to leave his van. Obviously, the well had to be studied and measurements taken, and by then it was time for lunch. Post Office business would be resumed at two o'clock.

A couple of days later, I was summoned from the house by a car horn, and found the dogs circling a new white Mercedes. The driver wasn't prepared to leave the safety of his car, but risked a half-open window. I looked in and saw a small brown couple beaming at me nervously. They complimented me on the ferocity of the dogs and requested permission to get out. They were both dressed for the city, the man in a sharply-cut suit, his wife in hat and cloak and patent leather boots.

How fortunate to find me at home, they said, and what a beautiful house. Had I lived here long? No? Then I would undoubtedly be needing some genuine Oriental carpets. This was indeed my lucky day, because they had just come from an important carpet exhibition in Avignon, and by chance a few choice items remained unsold. Before taking them up to Paris – where people of taste would fight to buy them – the couple had decided to take a drive in the country, and fate had led them to me. To mark the happy occasion, they were prepared to let me choose from their most exquisite treasures at what they described as *very interesting* prices.

While the natty little man had been telling me the good news, his wife had been unloading carpets from the car and arranging them artistically up and down the drive, commenting loudly on the charms of each one: 'Ah, what a beauty!' and 'See the colours in the sun' and 'This one – oh, I shall be sad to see it go'. She trotted back to join us, patent boots twinkling, and she and her husband looked at me expectantly.

The carpet-seller does not enjoy a good reputation in Provence, and to describe a man as a *marchand de tapis* is to imply that he is at best shifty and at worst someone who would steal the corset from your grandmother. I had also been told that travelling carpet-sellers often acted as reconnaissance parties, spying out the land for their burglar associates. And there was always the possibility that the carpets would be fakes, or stolen.

But they didn't look like fakes, and there was one small rug that I thought was very handsome. I made the mistake of saying so, and Madame looked at her husband in well-rehearsed surprise. 'Extraordinary!' she said. 'What an eye Monsieur has. This is indisputably our favourite too. But why not have something a little bigger as well?' Alas, I said, I was penniless, but this was brushed aside as a minor and temporary inconvenience. I could always pay later, with a substantial discount for cash. I looked again at the rug. One of the dogs was lying on it, snoring gently. Madame crooned with delight. 'You see, Monsieur? The *toutou* has chosen it for you.' I gave in. After three minutes of inexpert haggling on my part, the original price was reduced by fifty per cent, and I went to fetch the cheque book. They watched closely while I made out the cheque, telling me to leave the payee's name blank. With a promise to return next year, they drove slowly round our new rug and the sleeping dog, Madame smiling and waving regally from her nest of carpets. Their visit had taken up the entire morning.

The final interruption ended the week on a sour note. A truck had come to deliver gravel and, as I watched it backing towards the spot the driver had chosen to unload, the rear wheels suddenly sunk into the ground. There was a crack, and the truck tilted backwards. A pungent and unmistakable smell filled the air. The driver got out to inspect the damage and said, with unconscious accuracy, the single most appropriate word for the occasion.

'*Merde!*' He had parked in the septic tank.

'So you see,' I said to our friend from Paris, 'one way or another, there's never a dull moment.'

He didn't reply, and I reached over and took off his sunglasses. The sun in his eyes woke him up.

'What?'

* * * * *

MAY

Le premier Mai started well, with a fine sunrise, and as it was a national holiday we thought we should celebrate in correct French fashion by paying homage to the summer sport and taking to our bicycles.

Tougher and more serious cyclists had been training for weeks, muffled against the spring winds in thick black tights and face masks, but now the air was warm enough for delicate amateurs like us to go out in shorts and sweaters. We had bought two lightweight and highly-strung machines from a gentleman in Cavaillon called Edouard Cunty – '*Vélos de Qualité!*' – and we were keen to join the brightly coloured groups from local cycling clubs as they swooped gracefully and without any apparent effort up and down the back country roads. We assumed that our legs, after a winter of hard walking, would be in good enough condition for a gentle ten-mile spin up to Bonnieux and over to Lacoste – an hour of light exercise to limber up, nothing too strenuous.

It was easy enough to begin with, although the narrow, hard saddles made an early impression, and we realised why some cyclists slip a pound of rump steak inside the back of their shorts to cushion the coccyx from the road. But for the first couple of miles there was nothing to do except glide along and enjoy the scenery. The cherries were ripening, the winter skeletons of the vines had disappeared under a cover of bright green leaves, the mountains looked lush and soft. The tyres made a steady thrumming sound, and there were occasional whiffs of rosemary and lavender and wild thyme. This was more exhilarating than walking, quieter and healthier than driving, not too taxing and altogether delightful. Why hadn't we done it before? Why didn't we do it every day?

The euphoria lasted until we began to climb up to Bonnieux. My bicycle suddenly put on weight. I could feel the muscles in my thighs complaining as the gradient became steeper, and my unseasoned backside was aching. I forgot about the beauties of nature and wished I had worn steak in my shorts. By the time we reached the village it hurt to breathe.

The woman who runs the Café Clerici was standing outside with her hands on her ample hips. She looked at the two red-faced, gasping figures bent over their handlebars. '*Mon Dieu!* The Tour de France is early this year.' She brought us beer, and we sat in the comfort of chairs designed for human bottoms. Lacoste now seemed rather far away.

The hill that twists up to the ruins of the Marquis de Sade's château was long and steep and agonising. We were half way up and flagging when we heard a whirr of *dérailleur* gears, and we were overtaken by another cyclist – a wiry, brown man who looked to be in his mid-sixties. '*Bon jour,*' he said brightly, '*bon vélo*', and he continued up the hill and out of sight. We laboured on, heads low, thighs burning, regretting the beer.

The old man came back down the hill, turned, and cruised along next to us. '*Courage,*' he said, not even breathing hard, '*c'est pas loin. Allez!*' And he rode with us into Lacoste, his lean old legs, shaved bare in case of falls and grazes, pumping away with the smoothness of pistons.

We collapsed on the terrace of another café, which overlooked the valley. At least it would be downhill most of the way home, and I gave up the idea of calling an ambulance. The old man had a peppermint *frappé*, and told us that he had done thirty kilometres so far, and would do another twenty before lunch. We congratulated him on his fitness. 'It's not what it was. I had to stop doing the Mont Ventoux ride when I turned sixty. Now I just do these little *promenades.*' Any slight satisfaction we felt at climbing the hill disappeared.

The ride back was easier, but we were still hot and sore when we reached home. We dismounted and walked stiff-legged to the pool, discarding clothes as we went, and dived in. It was like going to heaven. Lying in the sun afterwards with a glass of wine we decided that cycling would be a regular part of our summer lives. It was, however, some time before we could face the saddles without flinching.

* * * * *

The fields around the house were inhabited every day by figures moving slowly and methodically across the landscape, weeding the vineyards, treating the cherry trees, hoeing the sandy earth. Nothing was hurried. Work stopped at noon for lunch in the shade of a tree, and the only sounds for two hours were snatches of distant conversation that carried hundreds of yards on the still air.

Faustin was spending most of his days on our land, arriving just after seven with his dog and his tractor and usually contriving to organise his work so that it ended near the house – close enough to hear the sound of bottles and glasses. One drink to settle the dust and be sociable was his normal ration but, if the visit stretched to two drinks, it meant business – some new step forward in agricultural co-operation which he had been mulling over during his hours among the vines. He never approached a subject directly, but edged towards it, crabwise and cautious.

'Do you like rabbits?'

I knew him well enough to understand that he wasn't talking about the charms of the rabbit as a domestic pet, and he confirmed this by patting his belly and muttering reverently about *civets* and *pâtés*. But the trouble with rabbits, he said, was their appetites. They ate like holes, kilos and kilos. I nodded, but I was at a loss to know where our interests and those of the hungry rabbit coincided.

Faustin stood up and beckoned me to the door of the courtyard. He pointed at two small terraced fields. 'Lucerne,' he said. 'Rabbits love it. You could get three cuts from those fields between now and autumn.' My knowledge of local plant life was far from complete, and I had thought that the fields were covered in some kind of dense Provençal weed which I had been meaning to clear. It was fortunate I hadn't; Faustin's rabbits would never have forgiven me. It was an unexpected triumph for gardening by neglect. In case I had missed the point, Faustin waved his glass at the fields and said again, 'Rabbits love lucerne.' He made nibbling noises. I told him he could have as much as his rabbits could eat, and he stopped nibbling.

'*Bon*. If you're sure you won't need it.' Mission accomplished, he stumped off towards his tractor.

Faustin is slow in many ways, but quick with his gratitude. He was back the following evening with an enormous bouquet of asparagus, neatly tied with red, white and blue ribbon. His wife Henriette was behind him carrying a pickaxe, a ball of string and a tub filled with young lavender plants. They should have been planted long before, she said, but her cousin had only just brought them down from the Basses-Alpes. They must be planted at once.

Labour was divided rather unfairly, it seemed to us. Faustin was in charge of keeping the string straight and drinking pastis; Henriette swung the pickaxe, each planting hole a pick handle's distance from the next. Offers to help were refused. 'She's used to it,' said Faustin proudly, as Henriette swung and measured and planted in the twilight, and she laughed. 'Eight hours of this and you sleep like a baby.' In half an hour it was done – a bed of fifty plants that would be the size of hedgehogs in six months, knee-high in two years, arranged with meticulous symmetry to mark the boundary of the rabbits' lucerne factory.

Whatever had been on the menu for dinner was forgotten, and we prepared the asparagus. There was too much for one meal, more than I could get both hands around, the patriotic tricolour ribbon printed with Faustin's name and address. He told us that it was the law in France for the producer to be identified like this, and we hoped one day to have our own ribbon when our asparagus plants grew up.

The pale shoots were as fat as thumbs, delicately coloured and patterned at the tips. We ate them warm, with melted butter. We ate bread that had been baked that afternoon in the old *boulangerie* at Lumières. We drank the light red wine from the vineyards in the valley. We supported local industry with every mouthful.

Through the open door we could hear the croaking of our resident frog, and the long, sliding song of a nightingale. We took a final glass of wine outside and looked by the light of the moon at the new lavender bed while the dogs rooted for mice in the lucerne fields. The rabbits would eat well this summer and, Faustin had promised, would taste all the better for it in the winter. We realised we were becoming as obsessive about food as the French, and went back indoors to attend to some unfinished business with a goat's cheese.

* * * * *

Bernard the *pisciniste* had brought us a present, and he was assembling it with great enthusiasm. It was a floating armchair for the pool, complete with a drinks compartment. It had come all the way from Miami, Florida, which in Bernard's opinion was the capital of the world for pool accessories. 'The French don't understand these things,' he said disparagingly. 'There are companies making air cushions, but how can you drink on a floating cushion?' He tightened the last wing-nut on the frame and stood back to admire the chair in all its Miami dazzle, a vivid block of styrofoam, plastic and aluminium. 'There. The glass fits here in the arm-rest. You can repose in great comfort. *C'est une merveille.*' He launched the chair into the water, careful not to splash his pink shirt and white trousers. 'You must put it away every night,' he said. 'The gypsies will be here soon for the cherry-picking. They'll steal anything.'

It was a reminder that we had been intending to get some insurance arranged for the house, but with the builders making holes in the walls I couldn't imagine any insurance company taking the risk. Bernard removed his sunglasses in horror. Didn't we know? There was a higher burglary rate in the Vaucluse than anywhere else in France except Paris. He looked at me as if I had committed an act of terminal lunacy. 'You must be protected immediately. I will send a man this afternoon. Stay *en garde* until he comes.'

I thought this was perhaps a little dramatic, but Bernard seemed convinced that robber bands were lurking close by, waiting only for us to go to the village butcher before swooping down in a pantechnicon to pick the house bare. Only last week, he told me, he had found his car jacked up outside his own front door with all four wheels removed. These people were *salauds*.

One reason, apart from idleness, why we had neglected the matter of insurance was that we detested insurance companies, with their weasel words and evasions and extenuating circumstances, and their conditional clauses set in minuscule, illegible type. But Bernard was right. It was stupid to trust to luck. We resigned ourselves to spending the afternoon with a grey man in a suit who would tell us to put a lock on our refrigerator.

It was early evening when the car pulled up in a cloud of dust. The driver had obviously come to the wrong house. He was young and dark and good-looking, resplendent in the costume of a 1950s saxophone player – a wide-shouldered drape jacket shot through with gleaming threads, a lime-green shirt, capacious trousers that narrowed to hug his ankles, shoes of dark blue suede with bulbous crêpe soles, a flash of turquoise socks.

'Fructus, Thierry. *Agent d'assurance.*' He walked into the house with short, jaunty steps. I half expected him to start snapping his fingers and make a few mean moves across the floor. I offered him a beer while I got over my surprise, and he sat down and gave me the benefit of his vibrant socks.

'*Une belle mesong.*' He had a strong Provençal accent which contrasted strangely with the clothes, and which I found reassuring. He was businesslike and serious, and asked if we were living in the house all year round; the high rate of burglaries in the Vaucluse, he said, was partly due to the large number of holiday homes. When houses are left empty for ten months a year, well . . . the shoulders of his jacket escalated in an upholstered shrug. The stories one heard in his profession made you want to live in a safe.

But that needn't concern us. We were permanent. And, furthermore, we had dogs. This was good, and it would be taken into account when he assessed the premium. Were they vicious? If not, perhaps they could be trained. He knew a man who could turn poodles into lethal weapons.

He made some notes in a neat, small hand and finished his beer. We went on a tour of the house. He approved of the heavy wooden shutters and solid old doors, but stopped and sucked his teeth in

front of a small window – a *fenestron* that was less than a foot square. The modern professional burglar, he told us, will often work like Victorian chimney-sweeps used to, sending a child through openings that would be impossible for adults. Since we were in France, there was an official, established size for juvenile burglars; they were all more than 12 centimetres wide, and narrower gaps were therefore childproof. Quite how this had been calculated Monsieur Fructus didn't know, but the little window would have to be barred to make it safe from the depredations of anorexic five-year-olds.

For the second time that day, the itinerant cherry-pickers were held up as a threat to domestic security – Spaniards or Italians, Monsieur Fructus said, working for a pittance of three francs a kilo, here today and gone tomorrow, a grave risk. One cannot be too careful. I promised to stay on the alert and to barricade the window as soon as possible, and to talk to the dogs about being vicious. Reassured, he drove off into the sunset with the sound of Bruce Springsteen bellowing from the car stereo.

The cherry-pickers had started to hold an awful fascination for us. We wanted to see some of these light-fingered scoundrels in the flesh; surely it would be any day now that they would descend on us, because the cherries were certainly ready to pick. We'd tasted them. We now had breakfast on a small terrace which faced the early sun, twenty yards from an old tree bowed down with fruit. While my wife made coffee, I picked cherries. They were cool and juicy, almost black, and they were our first treat of the day.

We knew that organised picking had begun the morning we heard a radio playing somewhere between the house and the road. The dogs went to investigate, bristling and noisy with self-importance, and I followed, expecting to find a gang of swarthy strangers and their larcenous children. The leaves on the trees hid their bodies from the waist upwards. All I could see were various pairs of legs balanced on triangular wooden ladders, and then a great brown moon of a face under a straw trilby poked through the foliage.

'*Sont bonnes, les cerises.*' He offered me a finger, with a pair of cherries dangling from the end. It was Faustin. He and Henriette and assorted relatives had decided to gather the fruit themselves because of the wages demanded by outside labour. Someone had actually asked for five francs a kilo. Imagine! I tried to: an uncomfortable ten-hour working day perched on a ladder and tormented by fruit-flies, nights sleeping rough in a barn or the back of a van – it didn't sound like over-generous pay to me. But Faustin was adamant. It was daylight robbery, *mais enfin*, what could you expect from cherry-pickers? He reckoned to get about two tons of fruit for the jam factory in Apt, and the proceeds would be kept in the family.

The orchards were well-stocked with pickers of all shapes and sizes during the next few days, and I stopped to give two of them a ride into Bonnieux one evening. They were students from Australia, red from the sun and stained with cherry juice. They were exhausted, and complained about the hours and the tedium and the stinginess of the French peasant.

'Well, at least you're seeing a bit of France.'

'France?' said one of them. 'All I've seen is the inside of a flaming cherry tree.'

They were determined to go back to Australia with no good memories of their time in Provence. They didn't like the people. They were suspicious of the food. French beer gave them the runs. Even the scenery was small by Australian standards. They couldn't believe I had chosen to live here. I tried to explain, but we were talking about two different countries. I dropped them off at the café, where they would spend the evening being homesick. They were the only miserable Australians I had ever met, and it was depressing to hear a place that I loved being so thoroughly condemned.

Bernard cheered me up. I had come to his office in Bonnieux with the translation of a letter that he had received from an English client, and he was laughing as he opened the door.

His friend Christian, who was also our architect, had just been asked to re-design a brothel in Cavaillon. There were, *naturelle-ment*, many unusual requirements to be met. The placing of mirrors, for instance, was of crucial importance. Certain fittings not normally found in polite bedrooms would have to be accom-modated. The bidets would be working overtime, and they would have to function impeccably. I thought of Monsieur Menicucci and *jeune* trying to adjust their taps and washers while travelling salesmen from Lille chased scantily-clad young ladies through the corridors. I thought of Ramon the plasterer, a man with a definite twinkle in his eye, let loose among the *filles de joie*. He'd stay there for the rest of his life. It was a wonderful prospect.

Unfortunately, said Bernard, although Christian regarded it as an interesting architectural challenge, he was going to turn it down. Madame who ran the enterprise wanted the work finished in an impossibly short time, and she wasn't prepared to close the premises while it was being done, which would place severe demands on the workmen's powers of concentration. Nor was she prepared to pay the TVA, arguing that she didn't charge her clients a sales tax, so why should she have to pay one? In the end, she would hire a couple of renegade masons who would do a fast and clumsy job, and the chance of getting Cavaillon's brothel photographed for the pages of the *Architectural Digest* would be lost. A sad day for posterity.

* * * * *

We were learning what it was like to live more or less permanently with guests. The advance guard had arrived at Easter, and others were booked in until the end of October. Half-forgotten invitations, made in the distant safety of winter were coming home to roost and drink and sunbathe. The girl in the laundry assumed from our sheet count that we were in the hotel business, and we remembered the warnings of more experienced residents.

As it turned out, the early visitors must have taken a course in being ideal guests. They rented a car, so that they weren't dependent on us to ferry them around. They amused themselves during the day, and we had dinner together in the evening. They left when they had said they were going to. If they were all like that, we thought, the summer would pass very pleasantly.

The greatest problem, as we soon came to realise, was that our guests were on holiday. We weren't. We got up at seven. They were often in bed until ten or eleven, sometimes finishing breakfast just in time for a swim before lunch. We worked while they sunbathed. Refreshed by an afternoon nap, they came to life in the evening, getting into high social gear as we were falling asleep in the salad. My wife, who has a congenitally hospitable nature and a horror of seeing people underfed, spent hours in the kitchen, and we washed dishes far into the night.

Sundays were different. Everybody who came to stay with us wanted to go to one of the Sunday markets, and they start early. For once in the week, we and the guests kept the same hours. Bleary-eyed and unusually quiet, they would doze in the back of the car during the twenty-minute ride to breakfast in the café overlooking the river at Isle-sur-la-Sorgue.

We parked by the bridge and woke our friends. They had gone to bed, reluctant and still boisterous, at two in the morning, and the bright light was having savage effects on their hangovers. They hid behind sunglasses and nursed big cups of *café crème*. At the dark end of the bar, a *gendarme* swallowed a surreptitious pastis. The man selling lottery tickets promised instant wealth to anyone who hesitated by his table. Two overnight truck drivers with blue sandpaper chins attacked their breakfasts of steak and *pommes frites* and shouted for more wine. The fresh smell of the river came through the open door, and ducks trod water while they waited for crumbs to be swept off the terrace.

We set off for the main square, running the gauntlet between groups of sallow gypsy girls in tight, shiny black skirts selling lemons and long plaits of garlic, hissing at each other in competition. The stalls were crammed haphazardly along the street – silver jewellery next to flat wedges of salt cod, wooden barrels of gleaming olives, hand-woven baskets, cinnamon and saffron and vanilla, cloudy bunches of gypsophila, a cardboard box full of mongrel puppies, lurid Johnny Hallyday T-shirts, salmon pink corsets and brassières of heroic proportions, rough country bread and dark terrines.

A lanky blue-black Senegalese loped through the turmoil of the square, festooned with his stock of authentic African tribal leatherware, made in Spain, and digital watches. There was a roll of drums. A man in a flat-topped peaked hat, accompanied by a dog dressed in a red jacket, cleared his throat and adjusted his portable loudspeaker system to an unbearable whine. Another drum roll. '*Prix choc*! Lamb from Sisteron! Charcuterie! Tripe! Go at once to Boucherie Crassard, Rue Carnot. *Prix choc!*' He fiddled again with his loudspeaker and consulted a clip-board. He was the town's mobile broadcasting service, announcing everything from birthday greetings to the local cinema programmes, complete with musical effects. I wanted to introduce him to Tony from advertising; they could have had an interesting time comparing promotional techniques.

Three Algerians with deeply rutted brown faces stood gossiping in the sun, their lunches hanging upside down from their hands. The live chickens they were holding by the legs had a fatalistic air about them, as if they knew that their hours were numbered. Everywhere we looked, people were eating. Stallholders held out free samples – slivers of warm pizza, pink ringlets of ham, sausage dusted with herbs and spiced with green peppercorns, tiny, nutty cubes of nougat. It was a dieter's vision of hell. Our friends started asking about lunch.

We were hours away from lunch, and before that we had to see the non-edible side of the market, the *brocanteurs* with their magpie collections of bits and pieces of domestic history rescued from attics all over Provence. Isle-sur-la-Sorgue has been an antique dealers' town for years; there is a huge warehouse by the station where thirty or forty dealers have permanent pitches, and where you can find almost anything except a bargain. But it was too sunny a morning to spend in the gloom of a warehouse, and we stayed among the outside stalls under the plane trees where the purveyors of what they like to call *haut bric-à-brac* spread their offerings on tables and chairs or on the ground, or hung them from nails in the tree trunks.

Faded sepia postcards and old linen smocks were jumbled up with fistfuls of cutlery, chipped enamel signs advertising purgatives and pomade for unruly moustaches, fire irons and chamber pots, Art Deco brooches and café ashtrays, yellowing books of poetry and the inevitable Louis Quatorze chair, perfect except for a missing leg. As it got closer to noon the prices went down and haggling began in earnest. This was the moment for my wife, who is close to professional standard at haggling, to strike. She had been circling a small plaster bust of Delacroix. The dealer marked it down to seventy-five francs, and she moved in for the kill.

'What's your best price?' she asked the dealer.

'My *best* price, Madame, is a hundred francs. However, this now seems unlikely, and lunch approaches. You can have it for fifty.'

We put Delacroix in the car, where he gazed thoughtfully out of the back window, and we joined the rest of France as the entire country prepared itself for the pleasures of the table.

One of the characteristics which we liked and even admired about the French is their willingness to support good cooking, no matter how remote the kitchen may be. The quality of the food is more important than convenience, and they will happily drive for an hour or more, salivating en route, in order to eat well. This makes it possible for a gifted cook to prosper in what might appear to be the most unpromising of locations, and the restaurant we had chosen was so isolated that on our first visit we'd taken a map.

Buoux is barely large enough to be called a village. Hidden in the hills about ten miles from Bonnieux, it has an ancient Mairie, a modern telephone kiosk, fifteen or twenty scattered houses and the 'Auberge de la Loube', built into the side of the hill with an empty, beautiful valley below it. We had found it with some difficulty in the winter, doubting the map as we went deeper and deeper into the wilderness. We had been the only clients that night, eating in front of a huge log fire while the wind rattled the shutters.

There could hardly have been a greater contrast between that raw night and a hot Sunday in May. As we came round the bend in the road leading to the restaurant we saw that the small parking area was already full, half of it taken up by three horses tethered to the bumper of a decrepit Citroën. The restaurant cat sprawled on the warm roof tiles, looking speculatively at some chickens in the next field. Tables and chairs were arranged along the length of an open-fronted barn, and we could hear the ice buckets being filled in the kitchen.

Maurice the chef came out with four glasses of peach champagne, and took us over to see his latest investment. It was an old open carriage with wooden wheels and cracked leather seats, large enough for half a dozen passengers. Maurice was planning to organise horse-drawn coach excursions through the Lubéron, stopping, *bien sûr*, for a good lunch on the way. Did we think it was an amusing idea? Would we come? Of course we would. He gave us a pleased, shy smile and went back to his ovens.

He had taught himself to cook, but he had no desire to become the Bocuse of Buoux. All he wanted was enough business to allow him to stay in his valley with his horses. The success of his restaurant was based on value for money and good, simple food rather than flights of gastronomic fancy, which he called *cuisine snob*.

There was one menu, at 110 francs. The young girl who serves on Sundays brought out a flat basketwork tray and put it in the middle of the table. We counted fourteen separate hors d'oeuvres – artichoke hearts, tiny sardines fried in batter, perfumed *tabouleh*, creamed salt cod, marinated mushrooms, baby calamari, *tapenade*, small onions in a fresh tomato sauce, celery and chick peas, radishes and cherry tomatoes, cold mussels. Balanced on the top of the loaded tray were thick slices of pâté and gherkins, saucers of olives and cold peppers. The bread had a fine crisp crust. There was white wine in the ice bucket, and a bottle of Châteauneuf-du-Pape left to breathe in the shade.

The other customers were all French, people from the neighbouring villages dressed in their clean, sombre Sunday clothes, and one or two more sophisticated couples looking fashionably out of place in their bright boutique colours. At a big table in the corner, three generations of a family piled their plates high and wished each other *bon appétit*. One of the children, showing remarkable promise for a six-year-old gourmet, said that he preferred this pâté to the one he ate at home, and asked his grandmother for a taste of her wine. The family dog waited patiently by his side, knowing as all dogs do that children drop more food than adults.

The main course arrived – rosy slices of lamb cooked with whole cloves of garlic, young green beans and a golden potato and onion *galette*. The Châteauneuf-du-Pape was poured, dark and heady, 'a wine with shoulders', as Maurice had said. We abandoned plans for an active afternoon, and drew lots to see who would get Bernard's floating armchair.

The cheese was from Banon, moist in its wrapping of vine

89

leaves, and then came the triple flavours and textures of the dessert: lemon sorbet, chocolate tart and *crème anglaise* all sharing a plate. Coffee. A glass of *marc* from Gigondas. A sigh of contentment. Where else in the world, our friends wondered, could you eat so well in such unfussy and relaxed surroundings? Italy, perhaps, but very few other places. They were used to London, with its over-decorated restaurants, its theme food and its grotesque prices. They told us about a bowl of pasta in Mayfair that cost more than the entire meal each of us had just had. Why was it so difficult to eat well and cheaply in London? Full of easy after-lunch wisdom, we came to the conclusion that the English eat out less often than the French, and when they do they want to be impressed as well as fed; they want bottles of wine in baskets, and finger bowls, and menus the length of a short novel, and bills they can boast about.

Maurice came over and asked if his cooking had pleased us. He sat down while he did some addition on a scrap of paper. *'La douloureuse,'* he said, pushing it over the table. It came to just over 650 francs, or about what two people would pay for a smart lunch in Fulham. One of our friends asked him if he'd ever thought of moving somewhere more accessible, like Avignon or even Ménerbes. He shook his head. 'It's good here. I have everything I want.' He could see himself there and cooking in twenty-five years' time, and we hoped we would still be in a fit state to totter up and enjoy it.

On the way home, we noticed that the combination of food and Sunday has a calming influence on the French motorist. His stomach is full. He is on his weekly holiday. He dawdles along without being tempted by the thrills of overtaking on a blind bend. He stops to take the air and relieve himself in the bushes by the roadside, at one with nature, nodding companionably at passing cars. Tomorrow he will take up the mantle of the kamikaze pilot once again, but today it is Sunday in Provence, and life is to be enjoyed.

JUNE

The local advertising industry was in bloom. Any car parked near a market for longer than five minutes became a target for roving Provençal media executives, who swooped from windscreen to windscreen stuffing small, excitable posters under the wipers. We were constantly returning to our car to find it flapping with messages – breathless news of forthcoming attractions, unmissable opportunities, edible bargains and exotic services.

There was an accordion contest in Cavaillon, with the added delights of 'Les Lovely Girls Adorablement Déshabillées (12 Tableaux)' to entertain us in between numbers. A supermarket was launching Opération Porc, which promised every conceivable part of a pig's anatomy at prices so low that we would rub our eyes in disbelief. There were boules tournaments and bals dansants, bicycle races and dog shows, mobile discothèques complete with disc jokeys, firework displays and organ recitals. There was Madame Florian, claivoyant and alchemist, who was so confident of her supernatural powers that she provided a guarantee of satisfaction with every seance. There were the working girls – from Eve, who described herself as a delicious creature available for saucy rendezvous, to Mademoiselle Roz, who could realise all our fantasies over the telephone, a service that she proudly announced had been banned in Marseille. And there was, one day, a desperate and hastily-written note asking not for our money but for our blood.

The smudged photocopy told the story of a small boy who was waiting to go to America for a major operation, and who needed constant transfusions to keep him alive until the hospital could accept him. '*Venez nombreux et vite,*' said the note. The blood unit would be at the village hall in Gordes at eight the next morning.

When we arrived at 8.30 the hall was already crowded. A dozen beds were arranged along the wall, all occupied, and from the row of upturned feet we could see that a good cross-section of the local population had turned out, easily identified by their footwear: sandals and espadrilles for the shopkeepers, high heels for the young matrons, canvas ankle boots for the peasants and carpet slippers for their wives. The elder women kept a firm grip on their shopping baskets with one hand while they clenched and unclenched the other fist to speed the flow of blood into the plastic bags, and there was considerable debate about whose contribution was the darkest, richest and most nourishing.

We lined up for a blood test behind a thick-set old man with a florid nose, a frayed cap and overalls, who watched with amusement as the nurse made unsuccessful attempts to prick the toughened skin of his thumb.

'Do you want me to fetch the butcher?' he asked. She jabbed once more, harder. '*Merde.*' A swelling drop of blood appeared, and the nurse transferred it neatly into a small tube, added some liquid and shook the mixture vigorously. She looked up from the tube with a disapproving expression.

'How did you come here?' she asked the old man.

He stopped sucking his thumb. 'Bicycle,' he said, 'all the way from Les Imberts.'

The nurse sniffed. 'It astonishes me that you didn't fall off.' She looked at the tube again. 'You're technically drunk.'

'Impossible,' said the old man. 'I may have had a little red wine with breakfast, *comme d'habitude*, but that's nothing. And furthermore,' he said, wagging his bloodstained thumb under her nose, 'a measure of alcohol enriches the corpuscles.'

The nurse was not convinced. She sent the old man away to have a second breakfast, this time with coffee, and told him to come back at the end of the morning. He lumbered off grumbling, holding the wounded thumb before him like a flag of battle.

We were pricked, pronounced sober, and shown to our beds. Our veins were plumbed into the plastic bags. We clenched and unclenched dutifully. The hall was noisy and good-humoured, and people who would normally pass each other on the street without acknowledgement were suddenly friendly, in the way that often happens when strangers are united in their performance of a good deed. Or it might have had something to do with the bar at the end of the room.

In England, the reward for a bagful of blood is a cup of tea and a biscuit. But here, after being disconnected from our tubes, we were shown to a long table manned by volunteer waiters. What would we like? Coffee, chocolate, croissants, brioches, sandwiches of ham or garlic sausage, mugs of red or rosé wine? Eat up! Drink up! Replace those corpuscles! The stomach must be served! A young male nurse was hard at work with a corkscrew, and the supervising doctor in his long white coat wished us all *bon appétit*. If the steadily growing pile of empty bottles behind the bar was anything to go by, the appeal for blood was an undoubted success, both clinically and socially.

Some time later, we received through the post our copy of *Le Globule*, the official magazine for the blood donors. Hundreds of litres had been collected that morning in Gordes, but the other statistic that interested me – the number of litres that had been drunk – was nowhere to be found, a tribute to medical discretion.

* * * * *

Our friend the London lawyer, a man steeped in English reserve, was watching what he called the antics of the frogs from the Fin de Siècle café in Cavaillon. It was market day, and the pavement was a human traffic jam, slow-moving, jostling and chaotic.

'Look over there,' he said, as a car stopped in the middle of the street while the driver got out to embrace an acquaintance, 'they're always mauling each other. See that? *Men kissing*. Damned unhealthy, if you ask me.' He snorted into his beer, his sense of propriety outraged by such deviant behaviour, so alien to the respectable Anglo-Saxon.

It had taken me some months to get used to the Provençal delight in physical contact. Like anyone brought up in England, I had absorbed certain social mannerisms. I had learned to keep my distance, to offer a nod instead of a handshake, to ration kissing to female relatives and to confine any public demonstrations of affection to dogs. To be engulfed by a Provençal welcome, as thorough and searching as being frisked by airport security guards, was, at first, a startling experience. Now I enjoyed it, and I was fascinated by the niceties of the social ritual, and the sign language which is an essential part of any Provençal encounter.

When two unencumbered men meet, the least there will be is the conventional handshake. If the hands are full, you will be offered a little finger to shake. If the hands are wet or dirty, you will be offered a forearm or an elbow. Riding a bicycle or driving a car does not excuse you from the obligation to *toucher les cinq sardines*, and so you will see perilous contortions being performed on busy streets as hands grope through car windows and across handlebars to find each other. And this is only at the first and most restrained level of acquaintance. A closer relationship requires more demonstrative acknowledgement.

As our lawyer friend had noticed, men kiss other men. They squeeze shoulders, slap backs, pummel kidneys, pinch cheeks. When a Provençal man is truly pleased to see you, there is a real possibility of coming away from his clutches with superficial bruising.

The risk of bodily damage is less where women are concerned, but an amateur can easily make a social blunder if he miscalculates the required number of kisses. In my early days of discovery, I would plant a single kiss, only to find that the other cheek was being proffered as I was drawing back. Only snobs kiss once, I was told, or those unfortunates who suffer from congenital *froideur*. I then saw what I assumed to be the correct procedure – the triple kiss, left-right-left, so I tried it on a Parisian friend. Wrong again. She told me that triple-kissing was a low Provençal habit, and that two kisses were enough among civilised people. The next time I saw my neighbour's wife, I kissed her twice. *'Non,'* she said, *'trois fois.'*

I now pay close attention to the movement of the female head. If it stops swivelling after two kisses, I am almost sure I've filled my quota, but I stay poised for a third lunge just in case the head should keep moving.

It's a different but equally tricky problem for my wife, who is on the receiving end and has to estimate the number of times she needs to swivel, or indeed if she needs to swivel at all. One morning she heard a bellow in the street, and turned to see Ramon the plasterer advancing on her. He stopped, and wiped his hands ostentatiously on his trousers. My wife anticipated a handshake, and held out her hand. Ramon brushed it aside and kissed her three times with great gusto. You never can tell.

Once the initial greeting is over, conversation can begin. Shopping baskets and packages are put down, dogs are tied to café tables, bicycles and tools are leaned up against the nearest wall. This is necessary, because for any serious and satisfactory discussion both hands must be free to provide visual punctuation, to terminate dangling sentences, to add emphasis or simply to decorate speech which, as it is merely a matter of moving the mouth, is not on its own sufficiently physical for the Provençal. So the hands and the eternally eloquent shoulders are vital to a quiet exchange of views, and in fact it is often possible to follow the gist of a Provençal conversation from a distance, without hearing the words, just by watching expressions and the movements of bodies and hands.

There is a well-defined silent vocabulary, starting with the hand-waggle which had been introduced to us by our builders. They used it only as a disclaimer whenever talking about time or cost, but it is a gesture of almost infinite flexibility. It can describe the state of your health, how you're getting on with your mother-in-law, the progress of your business, your assessment of a restaurant or your predictions about this year's melon crop. When it is a subject of minor importance, the waggle is perfunctory, and is accompanied by a dismissive raising of the eyebrows. More serious matters – politics, the delicate condition of one's liver, the prospects for a local rider in the Tour de France – are addressed with greater intensity. The waggle is in slow motion, with the upper part of the body swaying slightly as the hand rocks, a frown of concentration on the face.

The instrument of warning and argument is the index finger, in one of its three operational positions. Thrust up, rigid and unmoving, beneath your conversational partner's nose, it signals caution – watch out, *attention*, all is not what it seems. Held just below face level and shaken rapidly from side to side like an agitated metronome, it indicates that the other person is woefully ill-informed and totally wrong in what he has just said. The correct opinion is then delivered, and the finger changes from its sideways motion into a series of jabs and prods, either tapping the chest if the unenlightened one is a man or remaining a few discreet centimetres from the bosom in the case of a woman.

Describing a sudden departure needs two hands: the left, fingers held straight, moves upwards from waist level to smack into the palm of the right hand moving downwards – a restricted version of the popular and extremely vulgar bicep crunch. (Seen at its best during midsummer traffic jams, when disputing drivers will leave their cars to allow themselves the freedom of movement necessary for a left-arm uppercut stopped short by the right hand clamping on the bicep.)

At the end of the conversation, there is the promise to stay in touch. The middle three fingers are folded into the palm and the hand is held up to an ear, with the extended thumb and little finger imitating the shape of a telephone. Finally, there is a parting handshake. Packages, dogs and bicycles are gathered up until the whole process starts all over again fifty yards down the street. It's hardly surprising that aerobics never became popular in Provence. People get quite enough physical exercise in the course of a ten-minute chat.

These and other everyday amusements of life in nearby towns and villages were not doing much for our spirit of exploration and adventure. With so many distractions on our doorstep, we were neglecting the more famous parts of Provence, or so we were told by our friends in London. In the knowledgeable and irritating manner of seasoned armchair travellers, they kept pointing out how conveniently placed we were for Nîmes and Arles and Avignon, for the flamingoes of the Camargue and the *bouillabaisse* of Marseille. They seemed surprised and mildly disapproving when we admitted that we stayed close to home, not believing our excuses that we could never find the time to go anywhere, never felt a compulsion to go church-crawling or monument-spotting, didn't want to be tourists. There was one exception to this rooted existence, and one excursion that we were always happy to make. We both loved Aix.

The corkscrew road we take through the mountains is too narrow for trucks and too serpentine for anyone in a hurry. Apart from a single farm building with its ragged herd of goats, there is nothing to see except steep and empty landscapes of grey rock and green scrub oak, polished into high definition by the extraordinary clarity of the light. The road slopes down through the foothills on the south side of the Lubéron before joining up with the amateur Grand Prix that takes place every day on the RN7, the *Nationale Sept* that has eliminated more motorists over the years than is comfortable to think about as one waits for a gap in the traffic.

The road leads in to Aix at the end of the most handsome main street in France. The Cours Mirabeau is beautiful at any time of the year, but at its best between spring and autumn, when the plane trees form a pale green tunnel five hundred yards long. The diffused sunlight, the four fountains along the centre of the Cours' length, the perfect proportions which follow da Vinci's rule to 'let the street be as wide as the height of the houses' – the arrangement of space and trees and architecture is so pleasing that you hardly notice the cars.

Over the years, a nice geographical distinction has evolved between work and more frivolous activities. On the shady side of the street, appropriately, are the banks and insurance companies and property agents and lawyers. On the sunny side are the cafés.

I have liked almost every café that I have ever been to in France, even the ratty little ones in tiny villages where the flies are more plentiful than customers, but I have a soft spot for the sprawling cafés of the Cours Mirabeau, and the softest spot of all for the Deux Garçons. Successive generations of proprietors have put their profits under the mattress and resisted all thoughts of redecoration, which in France usually ends in a welter of plastic and awkward lighting, and the interior looks much the same as it must have looked fifty years ago.

The ceiling is high, and toasted to a caramel colour by the smoke from a million cigarettes. The bar is burnished copper, the tables and chairs gleam with the patina bestowed by countless bottoms and elbows, and the waiters have aprons and flat feet, as all proper waiters should. It is dim and cool, a place for reflection and a quiet drink. And then there is the terrace, where the show takes place.

Aix is a university town, and there is clearly something in the curriculum that attracts pretty students. The terrace of the Deux Garçons is always full of them, and it is my theory that they are there for education rather than refreshment. They are taking a degree course in café deportment, with a syllabus divided into four parts.

One: the arrival

One must always arrive as conspicuously as possible, preferably on the back of a crimson Kawasaki 750 motor cycle driven by a young man in head-to-toe black leather and three-day stubble. It is not done to stand on the pavement and wave him goodbye as he booms off down the Cours to visit his hairdresser. That is for *gauche* little girls from the Auvergne. The sophisticated student is too busy for sentiment. She is concentrating on the next stage.

Two: the entrance

Sunglasses must be kept on until an acquaintance is identified at one of the tables, but one must not appear to be looking for company. Instead, the impression should be that one is heading into the café to make a 'phone call to one's titled Italian admirer, when – *quelle surprise!* – one sees a friend. The sunglasses can then be removed and the hair tossed while one is persuaded to sit down.

Three: ritual kissing

Everyone at the table must be kissed at least twice, often three times, and in special cases four times. Those being kissed should remain seated, allowing the new arrival to bend and swoop around the table, tossing her hair, getting in the way of the waiters and generally making her presence felt.

Four: table manners

Once seated, sunglasses should be put back on to permit the discreet study of one's own reflection in the café windows – not for reasons of narcissism, but to check important details of technique: the way one lights a cigarette, or sucks the straw in a Perrier *menthe*, or nibbles daintily on a sugar lump. If these are satisfactory, the glasses can be adjusted downwards so that they rest charmingly on the end of the nose, and attention can be given to the other occupants of the table.

This performance continues from mid-morning until early evening, and never fails to entertain me. I imagine there must be the occasional break for academic work in between these hectic periods of social study, but I have never seen a textbook darken any of the café tables, nor heard any discussion of higher calculus or political science. The students are totally absorbed in showing form, and the Course Mirabeau is all the more decorative as a result.

It would be no hardship to spend most of the day café-hopping, but as our trips to Aix are infrequent we feel a pleasant obligation to squeeze in as much as possible during the morning – to pick up a bottle of *eau-de-vie* from the man in the rue d'Italie and some cheeses from Monsieur Paul in the rue des Marseillais, to see what new nonsense is in the windows of the boutiques which are crammed, chic by jowl, next to older and less transient establishments in the narrow streets behind the Cours, to join the crowds in the flower market, to take another look at the tiny, beautiful place d'Albertas, with its cobbles and its fountain, and to make sure that we arrive in the rue Fréderéric Mistral while there are still seats to be had at Chez Gu.

There are larger, more decorative and more gastronomically distinguished restaurants in Aix, but ever since we ducked into Gu one rainy day we have kept coming back. Gu himself presides over the room – a genial, noisy man with the widest, jauntiest, most luxuriant and ambitious moustache I have ever seen, permanently fighting gravity and the razor in its attempts to make contact with Gu's eyebrows. His son takes the orders and an unseen woman with a redoubtable voice – Madame Gu, perhaps – is audibly in charge of the kitchen. The customers are made up of local businessmen, the girls from Agnes B. round the corner, smart women with their shopping bags and dachshunds and the occasional furtive and transparently illicit couple murmuring intently and ignoring their *aioli*. The wine is served in jugs, a good three-course meal costs 80 francs, and all the tables are taken by 12.30 every day.

As usual, our good intentions to have a quick and restrained lunch disappear with the first jug of wine, and, as usual, we justify our self-indulgence by telling each other that today is a holiday. We don't have businesses to get back to or diaries full of appointments, and our enjoyment is heightened, in a shamefully unworthy way, by the knowledge that the people around us will be back at their desks while we are still sitting over a second cup of coffee and deciding what to do next. There is more of Aix to see, but lunch dulls the appetite for sightseeing, and our bag of cheeses would take a smelly revenge on the way home if they were jostled through the heat of the afternoon. There is a vineyard outside Aix that I have been meaning to visit. Or there is a curiosity that we noticed on the way into town, a kind of mediaeval junk yard, littered with massive relics and wounded garden statuary. There, surely, we will find the old stone garden bench we've been looking for, and they'll probably pay us to take it away.

Matériaux d'Antan takes up a plot the size of an important cemetery by the side of the RN7. Unusually, in a country so determined to safeguard its possessions from robbers that it has the highest padlock population in Europe, the site was completely open to the road: no fences, no threatening notices, no greasy Alsatians on chains and no sign of any proprietor. How trusting, we thought as we parked, to conduct a business without any obvious means of protecting the stock. And then we realised why the owner could afford to be so relaxed about security; nothing on display could have weighed less than five tons. It would have taken ten men and a hydraulic winch to lift anything, and a car transporter to take it away.

If we had been planning to build a replica of Versailles we could have done all our shopping there in one afternoon. A full-size bath, cut from a single slab of marble? Over in the corner, with brambles growing through the plug hole. A staircase for the entrance hall? There were three, of varying lengths, gracefully curved arrangements of worn stone steps, each step as large as a dining table. Great snakes of iron balustrading lay next to them, with or without the finishing touches of giant pineapples. There were entire balconies complete with gargoyles, marble cherubs the size of stout adults, who seemed to be suffering from mumps, terra-cotta amphorae eight feet long, lying in a drunken muddle on their sides, mill wheels, columns, architraves and plinths. Everything one could imagine in stone, except a plain bench.

'Bon jour.' A young man appeared from behind a scaled-up version of the Winged Victory of Samothrace and asked if he could help us. A bench? He hooked his index finger over the bridge of his nose while he thought, then shook his head apologetically. Benches were not his speciality. However, he did have an exquisite eighteenth-century gazebo in wrought iron, or, if we had a sufficiently large garden, there was a fine mock-Roman triumphal arch he could show us, ten metres high and wide enough for two chariots abreast. Such pieces were rare, he said. For a moment, we were tempted by the thought of Faustin driving his tractor through a triumphal arch on his way to the vineyard, a wreath of olive leaves round his straw trilby, but my wife could see the impracticalities of a 250-ton impulse purchase. We left the young man with promises to come back if we ever bought a château.

The answering machine welcomed us home, winking its little red eye to show that people had been talking to it. There were three messages.

A Frenchman whose voice I didn't recognise conducted a suspicious, one-sided conversation, refusing to accept the fact that he was talking to a machine. Our message, asking callers to leave a number where they could be reached, set him off. Why must I give you my number when I am already talking to you? He waited for a reply, breathing heavily. Who is there? Why do you not answer? More heavy breathing. *Allo? Allo? Merde. Allo?* His allotted span on the tape ran out while he was in mid-grumble, and we never heard from him again.

Didier, brisk and businesslike, informed us that he and his team were ready to resume work, and would be attacking two rooms at the bottom of the house. *Normalement*, they would certainly arrive tomorrow, or perhaps the day after. And how many puppies did we want? Pénélope had fallen pregnant to a hairy stranger in Goult.

And then there was an English voice, a man we remembered meeting in London. He had seemed pleasant, but we hardly knew him. This was about to change, because he and his wife were going to drop in. He didn't say when, and he didn't leave a number. Probably, in the way of the itinerant English, they would turn up one day just before lunch. But we'd had a quiet month so far, with few guests and fewer builders, and we were ready for a little company.

They arrived at dusk, as we were sitting down to dinner in the courtyard – Ted and Susan, wreathed in apologies and loud in their enthusiasm for Provence, which they had never seen before, and for our house, our dogs, us, everything. It was all, so they said several times in the first few minutes, super. Their breathless jollity was disarming. They talked in tandem, a seamless dialogue which neither required nor allowed any contribution from us.

'Have we come at a bad time? Typical of us, I'm afraid.'

'Absolutely typical. You must *loathe* people dropping in like this. A glass of wine would be lovely.'

'Darling, look at the pool. Isn't it *pretty*.'

'Did you know the post office in Ménerbes has a little map showing how to find you? *Les Anglais*, they call you, and they fish out this map from under the counter.'

'We'd have been here earlier, except that we bumped into this sweet old man in the village . . .'

'. . . well, his car, actually . . .'

'Yes, his car, but he was sweet about it, darling, wasn't he, and it wasn't really a shunt, more a scrape.'

'So we took him into the café and bought him a drink . . .'

'Quite a few drinks, wasn't it, darling?'

'And some for those funny friends of his.'

'Anyway, we're here now, and I must say it's *absolutely* lovely.'

'And so kind of you to put up with us barging in on you like this.'

They paused to drink some wine and catch their breath, looking around and making small humming noises of approval. My wife, acutely conscious of the slightest symptoms of undernourishment, noticed that Ted was eyeing our dinner, which was still untouched on the table. She asked if they would like to eat with us.

'Only if it's absolutely no trouble – just a crust and a scrap of cheese and maybe *one* more glass of wine.'

Ted and Susan sat down, still chattering, and we brought out sausage, cheeses, salad and some slices of the cold vegetable omelette called *crespaou* with warm, fresh tomato sauce. It was received with such rapture that I wondered how long it had been since their last meal, and what arrangements they had made for their next one.

'Where are you staying while you're down here?'

Ted filled his glass. Well, nothing had actually been booked – 'Typical of us, absolutely typical' – but a little *auberge*, they thought, somewhere clean and simple and not too far away because they'd adore to see the house in the daytime if we could bear it. There must be half a dozen small hotels we could recommend.

There were, but it was past ten, getting close to bedtime in Provence, and not the moment to be banging on shuttered windows and locked doors and dodging the attentions of hotel guard dogs. Ted and Susan had better stay the night and find somewhere in the morning. They looked at each other, and began a duet of gratitude that lasted until their bags had been taken upstairs. They cooed a final good night from the guest room window, and we could still hear them chirruping as we went off to bed. They were like two excited children, and we thought it would be fun to have them stay for a few days.

The barking of the dogs woke us just after three. They were

intrigued by noises coming from the guest room, heads cocked at the sound of someone being comprehensively sick, interspersed with groans and the splash of running water.

I always find it difficult to know how best to respond to other people's ailments. I prefer to be left alone when I'm ill, remembering what an uncle had told me long ago. 'Puke in private, dear boy,' he had said. 'Nobody else is interested in seeing what you ate.' But there are other sufferers who are comforted by the sympathy of an audience.

The noises persisted, and I called upstairs to ask if there was anything we could do. Ted's worried face appeared round the door. Susan had eaten something. Poor old thing had a delicate stomach. All this excitement. There was nothing to be done except to let nature take its course, which it then loudly did again. We retreated to bed.

The thunder of falling masonry started shortly after seven. Didier had arrived as promised, and was limbering up with a sawn-off sledgehammer and an iron spike while his assistants tossed sacks of cement around and bullied the concrete-mixer into life. Our invalid felt her way slowly down the stairs, clutching her brow against the din and the bright sunlight, but insisting that she was well enough for breakfast. She was wrong, and had to leave the table hurriedly to return to the bathroom. It was a perfect morning with no wind, no clouds and a sky of true blue. We spent it finding a doctor who would come to the house, and then went shopping for suppositories in the pharmacy.

Over the next four or five days, we came to know the chemist well. The unlucky Susan and her stomach were at war. Garlic made her bilious. The local milk, admittedly rather curious stuff, put her bowels in an uproar. The oil, the butter, the water, the wine – nothing agreed with her, and twenty minutes in the sun turned her into a walking blister. She was allergic to the South.

It's not uncommon. Provence is such a shock to the Northern system; everything is full-blooded. Temperatures are extreme, ranging from over a hundred degrees down to minus twenty. Rain, when it comes, falls with such abandon that it washes roads away and closes the autoroute. The Mistral is a brutal, exhausting wind, bitter in winter and harsh and dry in summer. The food is full of strong, earthy flavours that can overwhelm a digestion used to a less assertive diet. The wine is young and deceptive, easy to drink but sometimes higher in alcoholic content than older wines that are treated with more caution. The combined effects of the food and climate, so different from England, take time to get used to. There is nothing bland about Provence, and it can poleaxe people as it had poleaxed Susan. She and Ted left us to convalesce in more temperate surroundings.

Their visit made us realise how fortunate we were to have the constitutions of goats and skins that accepted the sun. The routine of our days had changed, and we were living outdoors. Getting dressed took thirty seconds. There were fresh figs and melons for breakfast, and errands were done early, before the warmth of the sun turned to heat in mid-morning. The flagstones round the pool were hot to the touch, the water still cool enough to bring us up from the first dive with a gasp. We slipped into the habit of that sensible Mediterranean indulgence, the siesta.

The wearing of socks was a distant memory. My watch stayed in a drawer, and I found that I could more or less tell the time by the position of the shadows in the courtyard, although I seldom knew what the date was. It didn't seem important. I was turning into a contented vegetable, maintaining sporadic contact with real life through telephone conversations with people in faraway offices. They always asked wistfully what the weather was like, and were not pleased with the answer. They consoled themselves by warning me about skin cancer and the addling effect of sun on the brain. I didn't argue with them; they were probably right. But, addled, wrinkled and potentially cancerous as I might have been, I had never felt better.

The masons were working stripped to the waist, enjoying the weather as much as we were. Their main concession to the heat was a slightly extended lunch break, which was monitored to the minute by our dogs. At the first sound of hampers being opened and plates and cutlery coming out, they would cross the courtyard at a dead run and take their places by the table, something they never did with us. Patient and unblinking, they would watch every mouthful with underprivileged expressions. Invariably, it worked. At the end of lunch they would skulk back to their lairs under the rosemary hedge, their cheeks bulging guiltily with Camembert or *cous-cous*. Didier claimed that it fell off the table.

Work on the house was going according to schedule – that is, each room was taking three months from the day the masons moved in to the day that we could move in. And we had the prospect of Menicucci and his radiators to look forward to in August. In another place, in less perfect weather, it would have been depressing, but not here. The sun was a great tranquilliser, and time passed in a haze of well-being; long, slow, almost torpid days when it was so enjoyable to be alive that nothing else mattered. We had been told that the weather often continued like this until the end of October. We had also been told that July and August were the two months when sensible residents left Provence for somewhere quieter and less crowded, like Paris. Not us.

JULY

My friend had rented a house in Ramatuelle, a few kilometres from Saint-Tropez. We wanted to see each other, despite a mutual reluctance to brave the bad-tempered congestion of high summer traffic. I lost the toss, and said I'd be there by lunchtime.

After driving for half an hour I found myself in a different country, inhabited mostly by caravans. They were wallowing towards the sea in monstrous shoals, decked out with curtains of orange and brown and window stickers commemorating past migrations. Groups of them rested in the parking areas by the side of the autoroute, shimmering with heat. Their owners, ignoring the open countryside behind them, set up picnic tables and chairs with a close and uninterrupted view of the passing trucks, and within easy breathing distance of the diesel fumes. As I turned off the autoroute to go down to Sainte-Maxime, I could see more caravans stretching ahead in a bulbous, swaying convoy, and I gave up any thoughts of an early lunch. The final five kilometres of the journey took an hour and a half. Welcome to the Côte d'Azur.

It used to be beautiful, and rare and expensive pockets of it still are. But compared with the peace and relative emptiness of the

Lubéron it seemed like a madhouse, disfigured by overbuilding, overcrowding and overselling: villa developments, *steack pommes frites*, inflatable rubber boats, genuine Provençal souvenirs made from olive wood, pizzas, water-skiing lessons, night clubs, go-kart tracks – the posters were everywhere, offering everything.

The people whose business it is to make a living from the Côte d'Azur have a limited season, and their eagerness to take your money before autumn comes and the demand for inflatable rubber boats stops is palpable and unpleasant. Waiters are impatient for their tips, shopkeepers snap at your heels so that you won't take too long to make up your mind, and then refuse to accept 200-franc notes because there are so many forgeries. A hostile cupidity hangs in the air, as noticeable as the smell of Ambre Solaire and garlic. Strangers are automatically classified as tourists and treated like nuisances, inspected with unfriendly eyes and tolerated for cash. According to the map, this was still Provence. It wasn't the Provence I knew.

My friend's house was in the pine forests outside Ramatuelle, at the end of a long private track, completely detached from the lunacy three kilometres away on the coast. He was not surprised to hear that a two-hour drive had taken more than four hours. He told me that to be sure of a parking spot for dinner in Saint-Tropez it was best to be there by 7.30 in the morning, that going down to the beach was an exercise in frustration and that the only guaranteed way to get to Nice airport in time to catch a plane was by helicopter.

As I drove back home in the evening against the caravan tide, I wondered what it was about the Côte d'Azur that continued to attract such hordes every summer. From Marseille to Monte Carlo, the roads were a nightmare and the sea shore was covered in a living carpet of bodies broiling in the sun, flank to oily flank for mile after mile. Selfishly, I was glad they wanted to spend their holidays there rather than in the open spaces of the Lubéron, among more agreeable natives.

Some natives, of course, were less agreeable than others, and I met one the next morning. Massot was *en colère*, kicking at the undergrowth in the small clearing near his house and chewing at his moustache in vexation.

'You see this?' he said. 'Those *salauds*. They come like thieves in the night and leave early in the morning. *Saloperie* everywhere.' He showed me two empty sardine cans and a wine bottle which proved beyond any reasonable doubt that his arch-enemies the German campers had been trespassing in his private section of the national park. That in itself was bad enough, but the campers had treated his elaborate defence system with contempt, rolling back boulders to make a gap in the barricade and – *sales voleurs!* – stealing the notices that warned of the presence of vipers.

Massot took off his jungle cap and rubbed the bald spot on the back of his head as he considered the enormity of the crime. He looked in the direction of his house, standing on tiptoe first on one side of the path, then on the other. He grunted.

'It might work,' he said, 'but I'd have to cut down the trees.'

If he removed the small forest that stood between his house and the clearing, he would be able to see the headlights of any car coming down the track and loose off a couple of warning shots from his bedroom window. But, then again, those trees were extremely valuable, and added to the general desirability of the house he was trying to sell. No buyer had yet been found, but it was only a matter of time before somebody recognised it for the bargain it was. The trees had better stay. Massot thought again, and suddenly brightened up. Maybe the answer was *pièges à feu*. Yes, he liked that.

I had heard about *pièges à feu*, and they sounded horrendous – concealed snares that exploded when they were disturbed, like miniature mines. The thought of fragments of German camper flying through the air was alarming to me, but clearly very amusing to Massot, who was pacing round the clearing saying *boum!* every three or four yards as he planned his minefield.

Surely he wasn't serious, I said, and in any case I thought that *pièges à feu* were illegal. Massot stopped his explosions and tapped the side of his nose, sly and conspiratorial.

'That may be true,' he said, 'but there's no law against notices.' He grinned, and raised both arms above his head. '*Boum!*'

Where were you twenty years ago, I thought, when they needed you on the Côte d'Azur?

Perhaps Massot's anti-social instincts were being intensified by the heat. It was often in the nineties by mid-morning, and the sky turned from blue to a burnt white by noon. Without consciously thinking about it, we adjusted to the temperature by getting up earlier and using the cool part of the day to do anything energetic. Any sudden or industrious activity between midday and early evening was out of the question; like the dogs, we sought out the shade instead of the sun. Cracks appeared in the earth, and the grass gave up trying to grow. For long periods during the day the only sounds were those made by the *cigales* round the house, the bees in the lavender and bodies toppling into the pool.

I walked the dogs each morning between six and seven, and they discovered a new sport, more rewarding than chasing rabbits and squirrels. It had started when they came across what they thought was a large animal made of bright blue nylon. Circling it at a safe distance, they barked until it stirred and finally woke. A rumpled face appeared from one end, followed a few moments later by a hand offering a biscuit. From then on, the sight of a sleeping bag among the trees meant food. For the campers, it must have been disquieting to wake up and see two whiskery faces only inches away, but they were amiable enough about it once they had recovered from the shock.

Strangely enough, Massot was half right. They were mostly Germans, but not the indiscriminate rubbish-tippers that he complained about. These Germans left no trace; everything was bundled into giant backpacks before they shuffled off like two-legged snails into the heat of the day. In my short experience of litter in the Lubéron, the French themselves were the most likely offenders, but no Frenchman would accept that. At any time of the year, but particularly in the summer, it was well known that foreigners of one stripe or another were responsible for causing most of the problems in life.

The Belgians, so it was said, were to blame for the majority of accidents because of their habit of driving in the middle of the road, forcing the famously prudent French driver into ditches to avoid being *écrasé*. The Swiss and the non-camping section of the German population were guilty of monopolising hotels and restaurants and pushing up property prices. And the English – ah, the English. They were renowned for the frailty of their digestive systems and their preoccupation with drains and plumbing. 'They have a talent for diarrhoea,' a French friend observed. 'If an Englishman hasn't got it, he is looking for somewhere to have it.'

There is just enough of a hint of truth in these national insults to sustain their currency, and I was witness to an interlude in one of Cavaillon's busiest cafés which must have confirmed the French in their opinion of English sensitivities.

A couple with their small son were having coffee, and the boy indicated his need to go to the lavatory. The father looked up from his two-day-old copy of the *Daily Telegraph*.

'You'd better make sure it's all right,' he said to the boy's mother. 'Remember what happened in Calais?'

The mother sighed, and made her way dutifully into the gloom at the rear of the café. When she reappeared it was at high speed, and she looked as if she had just eaten a lemon.

'It's *disgusting*. Roger is not to go in there.'

Roger became immediately interested in exploring a forbidden lavatory.

'I've got to go,' he said, and played his trump card. 'It's number two. I've got to go.'

'There isn't even a seat. It's just a *hole*.'

'I don't care. I've got to go.'

'You'll have to take him,' said the mother. 'I'm not going in there again.'

The father folded his newspaper and stood up, with young Roger tugging at his hand.

'You'd better take the newspaper,' said the mother.

'I'll finish it when I get back.'

'*There's no paper*,' she hissed.

'Ah. Well, I'll try to save the crossword.'

The minutes passed, and I was wondering if I could ask the mother exactly what had happened in Calais, when there was a loud exclamation from the back of the café.

'*Poo!*'

It was the emerging Roger, followed by his ashen-faced father holding the remnants of his newspaper. Conversation in the café stopped as Roger gave an account of the expedition at the top of his voice. The *patron* looked at his wife and shrugged. Trust the

English to make a spectacle out of a simple visit to the *wa-wa*.

The equipment that had caused such consternation to Roger and his parents was a *toilette à la Turque*, which is a shallow porcelain tray with a hole in the middle and foot-rests at each side. It was designed, presumably by a Turkish sanitary engineer, for maximum inconvenience, but the French had added a refinement of their own – a high-pressure flushing device of such velocity that unwary users can find themselves soaked from the shins down. There are two ways of avoiding sodden feet: the first is to operate the flushing lever from the safety of dry land in the doorway, but since this requires long arms and the balance of an acrobat, the second option – not to flush at all – is unfortunately much more prevalent. To add to the problem, some establishments install an energy-saving device which is peculiar to the French. The light switch, always located on the outside of the lavatory door, is fitted with an automatic timer that plunges the occupant into darkness after thirty-eight seconds, thus saving precious electricity and discouraging loiterers.

Amazingly enough, *à la Turque* lavatories are still being manufactured, and the most modern café is quite likely to have a chamber of horrors in the back. But, when I mentioned this to Monsieur Menicucci, he leapt to the defence of French sanitary ware, insisting that at the other end of the scale were lavatories of such sophistication and ergonometric perfection that *even an American* would be impressed. He suggested a meeting to discuss two lavatories we needed for the house. He had some marvels to show us, he said, and we would be ravished by the choice.

He arrived with a valise full of catalogues, and unloaded them on to the table in the courtyard as he made some mystifying remarks about vertical or horizontal evacuation. As he had said, there was a wide choice, but they were all aggressively modern in design and colour – squat, sculptural objects in deep burgundy or burnt apricot. We were looking for something simple and white.

'*C'est pas facile,*' he said. People nowadays wanted new forms and colours. It was all part of the French sanitary revolution. The traditional white was not favoured by the designers. There was, however, one model he had seen recently which might be exactly what we wanted. He rummaged through his catalogues and – yes, he was sure of it – this was the one for us.

'*Voilà! La W.C. haute couture!*' He pushed the catalogue over to us and there, lit and photographed like an Etruscan vase, was the Pierre Cardin lavatory.

'You see?' said Menicucci. 'It is even signed by Cardin.' And so it was, up on the top and well out of harm's way. Apart from the signature it was perfect, a handsome design that looked like a lavatory and not like a giant goldfish bowl. We ordered two.

It was a saddened Menicucci who telephoned a week later to tell us that the House of Cardin no longer made our lavatories. *Une catastrophe* but he would continue his researches.

A further ten days passed before he reappeared, now in triumph, coming up the steps to the house waving another catalogue above his head.

'*Toujours couture!*' he said. '*Toujours couture!*'

Cardin may have left the bathroom, but his place had been taken by the gallant Courrèges, whose design was very similar and who had exercised remarkable restraint in the matter of the signature, leaving it off altogether. We congratulated Menicucci, and he allowed himself a celebratory Coca-Cola. He raised his glass.

'Today the lavatories, tomorrow the central heating,' he said, and we sat for a while in the 90-degrees sunshine while he told us how warm we were going to be and went through his plan of attack. Walls were to be broken, dust would be everywhere, the noise of the jackhammer would take over from the bees and the crickets. There was only one bright spot about it, said Menicucci. It would keep the guests away for a few weeks. *Eh, oui.*

But before this period of enforced and ear-splitting seclusion we were expecting one last guest, a man so maladroit and disaster-prone, so absent-minded and undomesticated, so consistently involved in household accidents that we had specifically asked him to come on the eve of demolition so that the debris of his visit could be buried under the rubble of August. It was Bennett, a close friend for fifteen years who cheerfully admitted to being the World's Worst Guest. We loved him, but with apprehension.

He called from the airport, several hours after he was due to arrive. Could I come down and pick him up? There had been a slight problem with the car hire company, and he was stranded.

I found him in the upstairs bar at Marignane, comfortably installed with a bottle of champagne and a copy of the French edition of *Playboy*. He was in his late forties, slim and extremely good-looking, dressed in an elegant suit of off-white linen with badly scorched trousers. 'Sorry to drag you out,' he said, 'but they've run out of cars. Have some champagne.'

He told me what had happened and, as usual with Bennett, it was all so unlikely that it had to be true. The plane had arrived on time, and the car he had reserved, a convertible, was waiting for him. The top was down, it was a glorious afternoon and Bennett, in an expansive mood, had lit a cigar before heading towards the autoroute. It had burned quickly, as cigars do when fanned by a strong breeze, and Bennett had tossed it away after twenty minutes. He became aware that passing motorists were waving at him, so in return he waved to them; how friendly the French have become, he thought. He was some miles up the autoroute before he realised that the back of the car was burning, set on fire by the discarded cigar butt that had lodged in the upholstery. With what he thought was tremendous presence of mind, he pulled on to the hard shoulder, stood up on the front seat and urinated into the flames. And that was when the police had found him.

'They were terribly nice,' he said, 'but they thought it would be best if I brought the car back to the airport, and then the car rental people had a fit and wouldn't give me another one.'

He finished his champagne and gave me the bill. What with all the excitement, he said, he hadn't managed to change his traveller's cheques. It was good to see him again, still the same as ever, charming, terminally clumsy, beautifully dressed, permanently short of funds. My wife and I had once pretended to be his maid and manservant at a dinner party when we were all so broke that we shared out the tip afterwards. We always had fun with Bennett, and dinner that night lasted into the early hours of the morning.

The week passed as uneventfully as could be expected, given that our guest was a man who could, and often did, spill his drink over himself while looking at his watch, and whose immaculate white trousers never survived the first course of dinner unsoiled.

There were one or two breakages, the odd drowned towel in the swimming pool, a sudden panic when he realised that he had sent his passport to the dry cleaners, some worrying moments when he thought he had eaten a wasp, but no true calamities. We were sad to see him go, and hoped he would come back soon to finish the four half empty glasses of Calvados we found under his bed, and to pick up the underpants that he had left hanging decoratively from the hat rack.

* * * * *

It was Bernard who had told us about the old station café in Bonnieux. Solid and serious was how he described it, a family restaurant of the kind that used to exist all over France before food became fashionable and *bistrots* started serving slivers of duckling instead of *daube* and tripe. Go soon, Bernard said, because *la patronne* talks about retiring, and take a big appetite with you. She likes to see clean plates.

The station at Bonnieux has been closed for more than forty years, and the path that leads to it is potholed and neglected. From the road there is nothing to see – no signs, no menus. We had passed by dozens of times, assuming that the building was unoccupied, not knowing that a crowded car park was hidden behind the trees.

We found a space between the local ambulance and a mason's scarred truck, and stood for a moment listening to the clatter of dishes and the murmur of conversation that came through the open windows. The restaurant was fifty yards from the station, foursquare and unpretentious, with faded lettering just legible in hand-painted capitals: Café de la Gare.

A small Renault van pulled into the car park, and two men in overalls got out. They washed their hands at the old sink against the outside wall, using the yellow banana of soap that was mounted over the taps on its bracket, and elbowed the door open, hands still wet. They were regulars, and went straight to the towel which hung from a hook at the end of the bar. By the time they had dried their hands two glasses of pastis and a jug of water were waiting for them.

It was a big, airy room, dark at the front and sunny at the back, where windows looked over fields and vineyards towards the hazy bulk of the Lubéron. There must have been forty people, all men, already eating. It was only a few minutes past noon, but the Provençal has a clock in his stomach, and lunch is his sole concession to punctuality. *On mange à midi*, and not a moment later.

Each table had its white paper cover and two unlabelled bottles of wine, a red and a pink, from the Bonnieux co-operative two hundred yards away on the other side of the road. There was no written menu. Madame cooked five meals a week, lunch from Monday to Friday, and customers ate what she decided they would eat. Her daughter brought us a basket of good, chewy bread, and asked us if we wanted water. No? Then we must tell her when we wanted more wine.

Most of the other customers seemed to know each other, and there were some spirited and insulting exchanges between the tables. An enormous man was accused of slimming. He looked up from his plate and stopped eating long enough to growl. We saw our electrician and Bruno who lays the stone floors eating together in a corner, and recognised two or three other faces that we hadn't seen since work had stopped on the house. The men were sunburned, looking fit and relaxed as if they had been on holiday. One of them called across to us.

'*C'est tranquille chez vous*? Peaceful without us?'

We said we hoped they would be coming back when work started again in August.

'*Normalement, oui.*' The hand waggled. We knew what that meant.

Madame's daughter returned with the first course, and explained that it was a light meal today because of the heat. She put down an oval dish covered with slices of *saucisson* and cured ham, with tiny gherkins, some black olives and grated carrots in a sharp marinade. A thick slice of white butter to dab on the *saucisson*. More bread.

Two men in jackets came in with a dog and took the last empty table. There was a rumour, so Madame's daughter said, that the older of the two men had been the French Ambassador to a country in the Middle East. *Un homme distingué*. He sat there among the masons and plumbers and truck drivers, feeding his dog small pieces of sausage.

Salad arrived in glass bowls, the lettuce slick with dressing, and with it another oval dish. Noodles in a tomato sauce and slices of roast loin of pork, juicy in a dark onion gravy. We tried to imagine what Madame would serve up in the winter, when she wasn't toying with these light meals, and we hoped that she would have second thoughts about retiring. She had taken up her position behind the bar, a short, comfortably proportioned woman, her hair still dark and thick. She looked as though she could go on for ever.

Her daughter cleared away, emptied the last of the red wine into our glasses and, unasked, brought another bottle with the cheese. The early customers were starting to leave to go back to work, wiping their moustaches and asking Madame what she proposed to give them tomorrow. Something good, she said.

I had to stop after the cheese. My wife, who has never yet been defeated by a menu, had a slice of *tarte au citron*. The room began to smell of coffee and Gitanes, and the sun coming through the window turned the smoke blue as it drifted above the heads of the three men sitting over thimble-sized glasses of *marc*. We ordered coffee and asked for a bill, but bills were not part of the routine. Customers settled up at the bar on the way out.

Madame told us what we owed. Fifty francs each for the food, and four francs for the coffee. The wine was included in the price. No wonder the place was full every day.

Was it really true she was going to retire?

She stopped polishing the bar. 'When I was a little girl,' she said, 'I had to choose whether to work in the fields or in the kitchen. Even in those days I hated the land. It's hard, dirty work.' She looked down at her hands, which were well-kept and surprisingly young-looking. 'So I chose the kitchen, and when I married we moved here. I've been cooking for thirty-eight years. It's enough.'

We said how sorry we were, and she shrugged.

'One becomes tired.' She was going to live in Orange, she said, in an apartment with a balcony, and sit in the sun.

It was two o'clock, and the room was empty except for an old man with white stubble on his leather cheeks, dipping a sugar lump into his Calvados. We thanked Madame for a fine lunch.

'*C'est normale,*' she said.

The heat outside was like a blow on the skull and the road back to the house was a long mirage, liquid and rippling in the glare, the leaves on the vines drooping, the farm dogs silent, the countryside stunned and deserted. It was an afternoon for the pool and the hammock and an undemanding book, a rare afternoon without builders or guests, and it seemed to pass in slow motion.

By the evening, our skins prickling from the sun, we were sufficiently recovered from lunch to prepare for the sporting event of the week. We had accepted a challenge from some friends who, like us, had become addicted to one of the most pleasant games ever invented, and we were going to try to uphold the honour of Ménerbes on the *boules* court.

Long before, during a holiday, we had bought our first set of *boules* after watching the old men in Roussillon spend an enjoyably argumentative afternoon on the village court below the post office. We had taken our *boules* back to England, but it is not a game that suits the damp, and they gathered cobwebs in a barn. They had been almost the first things we unpacked when we came to live in Provence. Smooth and tactile, they fitted into the palm of the hand, heavy, dense, gleaming spheres of steel that made a satisfying *chock* when tapped together.

We studied the techniques of the professionals who played every day next to the church at Bonnieux – men who could drop a *boule* on your toe from twenty feet away – and came home to practise what we had seen. The true aces, we noticed, bent their knees in a crouch and held the *boule* with the fingers curled round and the palm facing downwards, so that when the *boule* was thrown, friction from the fingers provided backspin. And there were the lesser elements of style – the grunts and encouragements that helped every throw on its way, and the shrugs and muttered oaths when it landed short or long. We soon became experts in everything except accuracy.

There were two basic types of delivery: the low, rolling throw that skittered along the ground, or the high-trajectory drop shot, aimed to knock the opponent's *boule* off the court. The precision of some of the players we watched was remarkable, and for all our crouching and grunting it would take years of applied effort before we would be welcomed to a serious court like the one in Bonnieux.

Boules is an essentially simple game, which a beginner can enjoy from the first throw. A small wooden ball, the *cochonnet*, is tossed up the court. Each player has three *boules*, identified by different patterns etched into the steel, and at the end of the round the closest to the *cochonnet* is the winner. There are different systems of scoring, and all kinds of local bye-laws and variations. These, if carefully planned, can be of great advantage to the home team.

We were playing on our own court that evening, and the game was therefore subject to Lubéron Rules:

1. Anyone playing without a drink is disqualified.
2. Incentive cheating is permitted.
3. Disputes concerning the distance from the *cochonnet* are mandatory. Nobody's word is final.
4. Play stops when darkness falls unless there is no clear winner, in which case blind man's *boules* are played until there is a torchlight decision or the *cochonnet* is lost.

We had gone to some trouble to construct a court with deceptive slopes and shallow hollows to baffle visitors, and had roughened the playing surface so that our luck would have a sporting chance against superior skill. We were quietly confident, and I had the added advantage of being in charge of the pastis; any signs of consistent accuracy from the visiting team would be countered by bigger drinks, and I knew from personal experience what big drinks did to one's aim.

Our opponents included a girl of sixteen who had never played before, but the other three had at least six weeks of practice between them, and were not to be treated lightly. As we inspected the playing surface, they made disparaging comments about its lack of regularity, complained about the angle of the setting sun and made a formal request for dogs to be banned from the court. The old stone roller was trundled up and down to humour them. Moistened fingers were held in the air to gauge the strength of the breeze, and play commenced.

There is a distinct, if slow, rhythm to the game. A throw is made, and play stops while the next to throw strolls up for a closer look and tries to decide whether to bomb or whether to attempt a low, creeping delivery that will sidle round the other *boules* to kiss the *cochonnet*. A contemplative sip of pastis is taken, the knees are flexed, the *boule* loops through the air, thuds to earth and rolls with a soft crunching sound to its resting place. There are no hurried movements and almost no sporting injuries. (One exception being Bennett, who had scored a broken roof tile and self-inflicted concussion of the toe during his first and last game.)

Intrigue and gamesmanship make up for the lack of athletic drama, and the players that evening behaved abominably. *Boules* were moved by stealth, with accidental nudges of the foot. Players poised to throw were distracted by comments on their stance, offers of more pastis, accusations of stepping over the throwing line, warnings of dogs crossing the court, sightings of imaginary grass snakes and conflicting bad advice from every side. There were no clear winners at half-time, when we stopped to watch the sunset.

To the west of the house, the sun was centred in the vee made by two mountain peaks in a spectacular display of natural symmetry. Within five minutes it was over, and we played on in the *crépuscule*, the French word that makes twilight sound like a skin complaint. Measuring distances from the *cochonnet* became more difficult and more contentious, and we were about to agree on a dishonourable draw when the young girl whose first game it was put three *boules* in a nine-inch group. Foul play and alcohol had been defeated by youth and fruit juice.

We ate out in the courtyard, the flagstones sun-warm under our bare feet, the candlelight flickering on red wine and brown faces. Our friends had rented their house to an English family for August, and they were going to spend the month in Paris on the proceeds. According to them, all the Parisians would be down in Provence, together with untold thousands of English, Germans, Swiss and Belgians. Roads would be jammed; markets and restaurants impossibly full. Quiet villages would become noisy and everyone without exception would be in a filthy humour. We had been warned.

We had indeed. We had heard it all before. But July had been far less terrible than predicted, and we were sure that August could be dealt with very easily. We would unplug the 'phone, lie dow by the pool and listen, whether we liked it or not, to the concerto for jackhammer and blowtorch, conducted by Maestro Menicucci.

AUGUST

'There is a strong rumour,' said Menicucci, 'that Brigitte Bardot has bought a house in Roussillon.' He put his spanner down on the wall and moved closer so that there was no chance of *jeune* overhearing any more of Miss Bardot's personal plans.

'She intends to leave Saint-Tropez.' Menicucci's finger was poised to tap me on the chest. 'And I don't blame her. Do you know' – tap, tap, tap went the finger – 'that at any given moment during any day in the month of August there are five thousand people making *pipi* in the sea?'

He shook his head at the unsanitary horror of it all. 'Who would be a fish?'

We stood in the sun sympathising with the plight of any marine life unfortunate enough to be resident in Saint-Tropez while *jeune* toiled up the steps carrying a cast-iron radiator, a garland of copper piping slung round his shoulders, his Yale University T-shirt dark with sweat. Menicucci had made a significant sartorial concession to the heat, and had discarded his usual heavy corduroy trousers in favour of a pair of brown shorts that matched his canvas boots.

It was the opening day of *les grands travaux*, and the area in front of the house resembled a scrapyard. Piled around an oily workbench of great antiquity were some of the elements of our central heating system – boxes of brass joints, valves, soldering guns, gas canisters, hacksaws, radiators, drilling bits, washers and spanners and cans of what looked like black treacle. This was only the first delivery; the water tank, the fuel tank, the boiler and the burner were still to come.

Menicucci took me on a guided tour of the components, emphasising their quality. '*C'est pas de la merde, ça.*' He then pointed out which walls he was going to burrow through, and full realisation of the weeks of dust and chaos ahead sunk in. I almost wished I could spend August in Saint-Tropez with the half-million incontinent holidaymakers already there.

They and millions more had come down from the north in the course of a single massively constipated weekend. Twenty-mile traffic jams had been reported on the autoroute at Beaune, and anyone getting through the tunnel at Lyon in less than an hour was considered lucky. Cars and tempers became overheated. The breakdown trucks had their best weekend of the year. Fatigue and impatience were followed by accidents and death. It was a traditionally awful start to the month, and the ordeal would be repeated four weeks later in the opposite direction during the exodus weekend.

Most of the invaders passed us by on their way to the coast, but there were thousands who made their way into the Lubéron, changing the character of markets and villages and giving the local inhabitants something new to philosophise about over their pastis. Café regulars found their usual places taken by foreigners, and stood by the bar grizzling over the inconveniences of the holiday season – the bakery running out of bread, the car parked outside one's front door, the strange late hours that visitors kept. It was admitted, with much nodding and sighing, that tourists brought money into the region. Nevertheless, it was generally agreed that they were a funny bunch, these natives of August.

It was impossible to miss them. They had clean shoes and indoor skins, bright new shopping baskets and spotless cars. They drifted through the streets of Lacoste and Ménerbes and Bonnieux in a sightseer's trance, looking at the people of the village as if they too were quaint rustic monuments. The beauties of nature were loudly praised every evening on the ramparts of Ménerbes, and I particularly liked the comments of an elderly English couple as they stood looking out over the valley.

'What a marvellous sunset,' she said.

'Yes,' replied her husband. 'Most impressive for such a small village.'

Even Faustin was in fine holiday humour. His work on the vines was finished for the time being, and there was nothing he could do but wait for the grapes to ripen and try out his repertoire of English jokes on us. 'What is it,' he asked me one morning, 'that changes from the colour of a dead rat to the colour of a dead lobster in three hours?' His shoulders started to shake as he tried to suppress his laughter at the unbearably funny answer. '*Les Anglais en vacances*,' he said, '*vous comprenez?*' In case I hadn't fully grasped the richness of the joke, he then explained very carefully that the English complexion was known to be so fair that the slightest exposure would turn it bright red. '*Même sous un rayon de lune*,' he said, shuddering with mirth, 'even a moonbeam makes them pink.'

Faustin in waggish mood early in the morning was transformed into Faustin the sombre by the evening. He had heard news from the Côte d'Azur, which he told to us with a terrible relish. There had been a forest fire near Grasse, and the Canadair planes had been called out. These operated like pelicans, flying out to sea and scooping up a cargo of water to drop on the flames inland. According to Faustin, one of the planes had scooped up a swimmer and dropped him into the fire, where he had been *carbonisé*.

Curiously, there was no mention of the tragedy in *Le Provençal*, and we asked a friend if he had heard anything about it. He looked at us and shook his head. 'It's the old August story,' he said. 'Every time there's a fire someone starts a rumour like that. Last year they said a water-skier had been picked up. Next year it could be a doorman at the Negresco in Nice. Faustin was pulling your leg.'

It was difficult to know what to believe. Odd things were possible in August, and so we were not at all surprised when some friends who were staying in a nearby hotel told us that they had seen an eagle at midnight in their bedroom. Well, perhaps not the eagle itself, but the unmistakable and huge *shadow* of an eagle. They called the man on night duty at the desk, and he came up to their room to investigate.

Did the eagle seem to come from the wardrobe in the corner of the room? Yes, said our friends. *Ah bon*, said the man, the mystery is solved. He is not an eagle. He is a bat. He has been seen leaving that wardrobe before. He is harmless. Harmless he may be, said our friends, but we would prefer not to sleep with a bat, and we would like another room. *Non*, said the man. The hotel is full. The three of them stood in the bedroom and discussed bat-catching techniques. The man from the hotel had an idea. Stay there, he said. I shall return with the solution. He reappeared a few minutes later, gave them a large aerosol can of fly-killer and wished them good night.

* * * * *

The party was being held in a house outside Gordes, and we had been asked to join a few friends of the hostess for dinner before the other guests arrived. It was an evening that we anticipated with mixed feelings – pleased to be invited, but far from confident about our ability to stay afloat in a torrent of dinner party French. As far as we knew, we were going to be the only English-speakers there, and we hoped we wouldn't be separated from each other by too many breakneck Provençal conversations. We had been asked to arrive at what for us was the highly sophisticated hour of nine o'clock, and we drove up the hill towards Gordes with stomachs rumbling at being kept waiting so late. The parking area behind the house was full. Cars lined the road outside for fifty yards, and every other car seemed to have a Parisian 75 number plate. Our fellow guests were not going to be a few friends from the village. We began to feel we should have worn less casual clothes.

We walked inside and found ourselves in magazine country, decorated by *House and Garden* and dressed by *Vogue*. Candlelit tables were arranged on the lawn and the terrace. Fifty or sixty people, cool and languid and wearing white, held glasses of champagne in jewelled fingers. The sound of Vivaldi came through the open doorway of a floodlit barn. My wife wanted to go home and change. I was conscious of my dusty shoes. We had blundered into a *soirée*.

Our hostess saw us before we could escape. She at least was reassuringly dressed in her usual outfit of shirt and trousers.

'You found somewhere to park?' She didn't wait for an answer. 'It's a little difficult in the road because of that ditch.'

We said it didn't seem at all like Provence, and she shrugged. 'It's August.' She gave us a drink and left us to mingle with the beautiful people.

We could have been in Paris. There were no brown, weathered faces. The women were fashionably pallid, the men carefully barbered and sleek. Nobody was drinking pastis. Conversation was, by Provençal standards, whisper-quiet. Our perceptions had definitely changed. At one time, this would have seemed normal. Now it seemed subdued and smart and vaguely uncomfortable. There was no doubt about it; we had turned into bumpkins.

We gravitated towards the least chic couple we could see, who were standing detached from the crowd with their dog. All three were friendly, and we sat down together at one of the tables on the terrace. The husband, a small man with a sharp, Norman face, told us that he had bought a house in the village twenty years before for 3,000 francs, and had been coming down every summer since then, changing houses every five or six years. He had just heard that his original house was back on the market, over-restored and decorated to death and priced at a million francs. 'It's madness,' he said, 'but people like *le tout Paris*' – he nodded towards the other guests – 'they want to be with their friends in August. When one buys, they all buy. And they pay Parisian prices.'

They had begun to take their places at the tables, carrying bottles of wine and plates of food from the buffet. The women's high heels sank into the gravel of the terrace, and there were some refined squeals of appreciation at the deliciously primitive setting – *un vrai dîner sauvage* – even though it was only marginally more primitive than a garden in Beverly Hills or Kensington.

The Mistral started, suddenly and most inconveniently, while there was still plenty of uneaten shrimp salad on the tables. Lettuce leaves and scraps of bread became airborne, plucked from plates and blown among the snowy bosoms and silk trousers, scoring the occasional direct hit on a shirt front. Table cloths snapped and billowed like sails, tipping over candles and wine glasses. Carefully arranged coiffures and composures were ruffled. This was a little too *sauvage*. There was a hasty retreat, and dinner was resumed under shelter.

More people arrived. The sound of Vivaldi from the barn was replaced by a few seconds of electronic hissing, followed by the shrieks of a man undergoing heart surgery without anaesthetic: Little Richard was inviting us to get down and boogie.

We were curious to see what effect the music would have on such an elegant gathering. I could imagine them nodding their heads in time to a civilised tune, or dancing in that intimate crouch the French adopt whenever they hear Charles Aznavour, but *this* – this was a great sweating squawk from the jungle. AWOPBOPALOOWOPAWOPBAMBOOM! We climbed the steps to the barn to see what they would make of it.

Coloured strobe lighting was flashing and blinking, synchronised with the drumbeat and bouncing off the mirrors propped against the walls. A young man, shoulders hunched and eyes half-closed against the smoke of his cigarette, stood behind the twin turntables, his fingers coaxing ever more bass and volume from the knobs on the console.

GOOD GOLLY MISS MOLLY! screamed Little Richard. The young man went into a spasm of delight, and squeezed out an extra decibel. YOU SURE LOVE TO BALL! The barn vibrated, and *le tout Paris* vibrated with it, arms and legs and buttocks and breasts jiggling and shaking and grinding and flailing around, teeth bared, eyes rolling, fists pumping the air, jewellery out of control, buttons bursting under the strain, elegant façades gone to hell as everyone writhed and jerked and twitched and *got down*.

Most of them didn't bother with partners. They danced with their own reflections, keeping one eye, even in the midst of ecstasy, fixed on the mirrors. The air was filled with the smell of warm and scented flesh, and the barn turned into one huge throb, seething and frenzied and difficult to cross without being spiked by elbows or lashed by a whirling necklace.

Were these the same people who had been behaving so decorously earlier in the evening, looking as though their idea of a wild time might be a second glass of champagne? They were bouncing away like amphetamine-stuffed teenagers, and they seemed set for the night. We dodged and sidestepped through the squirming mass and left them to it. We had to be up early in the morning. We had a goat race to go to.

We had first seen the poster a week before, taped to the window of a *tabac*. There was to be a *Grande Course de Chèvres* through the streets of Bonnieux, starting from the Café César. The ten runners and their drivers were listed by name. There were numerous prizes, bets could be placed and, said the poster, animation would be assured by a grand orchestra. It was clearly going to be a sporting event of some magnitude, Bonnieux's answer to the Cheltenham Gold Cup or the Kentucky Derby. We arrived well before the race to be sure of a good position.

By nine o'clock it was already too hot to wear a watch, and the terrace in front of the Café César was spilling over with customers having their breakfast of *tartines* and cold beer. Against the wall of the steps leading down to the rue Voltaire, a large woman had established herself at a table, shaded by a parasol that advertised *Véritable Jus de Fruit*. She beamed at us, riffling a book of tickets and rattling a cash box. She was the official bookmaker, although there was a man taking off-track bets in the back of the café, and she invited us to try our luck. 'Look before you bet,' she said. 'The runners are down there.'

We knew they weren't far away; we could smell them and their droppings, aromatic as they cooked in the sun. We looked over the wall, and the contestants looked back at us with their mad, pale eyes, masticating slowly on some pre-race treat, their chins fringed with wispy beards. They would have looked like dignified mandarins had it not been for the blue and white jockey caps that each of them was wearing, and their racing waistcoats, numbered to correspond with the list of runners. We were able to identify Bichou and Tisane and all the rest of them by name, but it was not enough to bet on. We needed inside information, or at least some help in assessing the speed and staying power of the runners. We asked the old man who was leaning on the wall next to us, confident in the knowledge that he, like every Frenchman, would be an expert.

'It's a matter of their *crottins*,' he said. 'The goats who make the most droppings before the race are likely to do well. An empty goat is faster than a full goat. *C'est logique.'* We studied form for a few minutes, and No. 6, Totoche, obliged with a generous effort. '*Voilà,*' said our tipster, 'now you must examine the drivers. Look for a strong one.'

Most of the drivers were refreshing themselves in the café. Like the goats, they were numbered and wore jockey caps, and we were able to pick out the driver of No. 6, a brawny, likely-looking man who seemed to be pacing himself sensibly with the beer. He and the recently emptied Totoche had the makings of a winning team. We went to place our bet.

'*Non.*' Madame the bookmaker explained that we had to get first, second and third in order to collect, which ruined our calculations. How could we know what the dropping rate had been while we were away looking at the drivers? A certainty had dwindled into a long shot, but we went for No. 6 to win, the only female driver in the race to come second and a goat called Nénette, whose trim fetlocks indicated a certain fleetness of hoof, to come in third. Business done, we joined the sporting gentry in the little *place* outside the café.

The grand orchestra promised by the poster – a van from Apt with a sound system in the back – was broadcasting Sonny and Cher singing 'I've Got You, Babe'. A thin, high-chic Parisienne we recognised from the night before started to tap one dainty white-shod foot, and an unshaven man with a glass of pastis and a heavy paunch asked her to dance, swivelling his substantial hips as an inducement. The Parisienne gave him a look that could have turned butter rancid, and became suddenly interested in the contents of her Vuitton bag. Aretha Franklin took over from Sonny and Cher, and children played hopscotch among the goat droppings. The *place* was packed. We wedged ourselves between a German with a video camera and the man with the paunch to watch as the finishing line was prepared.

A rope was strung across the *place*, about eight feet above the ground. Large balloons, numbered from one to ten, were filled with water and tied at regular intervals along the length of the rope. Our neighbour with the paunch explained the rules: each of the drivers was to be issued with a sharp stick, which had two functions. The first was to provide a measure of encouragement for any goats reluctant to run; the second was to burst their balloons at the end of the race to qualify as finishers. *Evidemment*, he said, the drivers would get soaked, which would be droll.

The drivers had now emerged from the café, and were swaggering through the crowd to collect their goats. Our favourite driver, No. 6, had his pocket knife out, and was putting a fine point on each end of his stick, which I took to be a good sign. One of the other drivers immediately lodged a complaint with the organisers, but the dispute was cut short by the arrival of a car which had somehow managed to creep down through one of the narrow streets. A young woman got out. She was holding a map. She looked extremely puzzled. She asked the way to the autoroute.

The way to the autoroute, unfortunately, was blocked by ten goats, two hundred spectators and a musical van. Nevertheless, said the young woman, that is where I am going. She got back in the car and started inching forward.

Consternation and uproar. The organisers and some of the drivers surrounded the car, banging on the roof, brandishing sticks, rescuing goats and children from certain death beneath the barely moving wheels. Spectators surged forward to see what was going on. The car, embedded in humanity, was forced to stop, and the young woman sat looking straight ahead, tight-lipped with exasperation. *Reculez!* shouted the organisers, pointing back in the direction the car had come from, and waving at the crowd to make way. With a vicious crunch of gears, the car reversed, whining angrily up the street to the sound of applause.

The contestants were called to the starting line, and drivers checked the fastening of the cords around the goats' necks. The goats themselves were unaffected by the drama of the occasion. No. 6 was trying to eat the waistcoat worn by No. 7. No. 9, our outsider, Nénette, insisted on facing backwards. The driver picked her up by her horns and turned her round, jamming her between his knees to keep her pointing in the right direction. Her jockey cap had been knocked over one eye, giving her a rakish and demented air, and we wondered about the wisdom of our bet. We were counting on her to take third place, but with impaired vision and no sense of geography this seemed unlikely.

They were under starter's orders. Weeks, maybe months, of training had prepared them for this moment. Horn to horn, waistcoat to waistcoat, they waited for the starting signal. One of the drivers belched loudly, and they were off.

Within fifty yards, it became apparent that these goats were not instinctive athletes, or else they had misunderstood the purpose of the event. Two of them applied their brakes firmly after a few yards, and had to be dragged along. Another remembered what it should have done half an hour before, and paused at the first bend to answer a call of nature. Nénette, possibly because she was half-blinkered by her cap, overshot the turn and pulled her driver into the crowd. The other runners straggled up the hill, stimulated by various methods of persuasion.

'Kick them up the arse!' shouted our friend with the paunch. The Parisienne, who was hemmed in next to us, winced. This encouraged him to give her the benefit of his local knowledge. 'Did you know,' he said, 'that the last one to finish gets eaten? Roasted on a spit. C'est vrai.' The Parisienne pulled her sunglasses from their nest in her hair and put them on. She didn't look well.

The course followed a circuit around the high part of the village, looping back down to the old fountain which had been transformed into a water obstacle with a plastic sheet stretched between some hay bales. This had to be waded or swum just before the final sprint to the line of balloons outside the café – a brutal test of co-ordination and stamina.

Progress reports were being shouted down by spectators at the half-way mark, and news reached us that No. 1 and No. 6 were fighting it out in the lead. Only nine goats had been counted going past; the tenth had *disparu*. 'Probably having its throat cut,' said the man with the paunch to the Parisienne. She made a determined effort, and pushed through the crowd to find less offensive company near the finishing line.

There was a splash from the fountain, and the sound of a woman's voice raised to scold. The water obstacle had claimed its first victim – a little girl who had miscalculated the depth, and who stood waist-deep in the water, bedraggled and bawling with surprise.

'*Ils viennent, les chèvres!*'

The girl's mother, in desperation at the thought of her child being trampled to a pulp by the contestants, hitched up her skirt and plunged into the water. 'What thighs!' said the man with the paunch, kissing the tips of his fingers.

With a clatter of hoofs, the leading runners approached the fountain and skidded into the hay bales, showing very little enthusiasm for getting wet. Their drivers grunted and cursed and tugged and finally manhandled their goats into the water and out the other side to the finishing straight, their sodden espadrilles squelching on the tarmac, their sticks poised like lances. The positions at half-way mark had been maintained, and it was still No. 1 and No. 6, Titine and Totoche, skittering up to the line of balloons.

No. 1, with an enormous backhand swipe, exploded his balloon first, showering the Parisienne, who stepped smartly backwards into a pile of droppings. No. 6, for all his stick-sharpening before the race, had more difficulty, just managing to burst his balloon before the next runners reached the line. One by one, or in dripping groups, they staggered in until all that remained was a single swollen balloon banging from the line. No. 9, the wayward Nénette, had not completed the course. 'The butcher's got her,' said the man with the paunch.

We saw her as we walked back to the car. She had broken her cord and escaped from her driver, and was perched high above the street in a tiny walled garden, her cap hanging from one horn, eating geraniums.

* * * * *

'*Bonjour, maçon.*'
'*Bonjour, plombier.*'
The team had arrived for another loud, hot day, and were exchanging greetings and handshakes with the formality of people who had never met before, addressing each other by *métier* rather than by name. Christian the architect, who had worked with them for years, never referred to them by their first names, but always by a rather grand and complicated hyphenation which combined surname with profession; thus Francis, Didier and Bruno became

Menicucci-Plombier, Andreis-Maçon and Trufelli-Carreleur. This occasionally achieved the length and solemnity of an obscure aristocratic title, as with Jean-Pierre the carpet layer, who was officially known as Gaillard-Poseur de Moquette.

They were gathered around one of many holes that Menicucci had made to accommodate his central heating pipes, and were discussing dates and schedules in the serious manner of men whose lives were governed by punctuality. There was a strict sequence to be followed: Menicucci had to complete laying his pipes; the masons were then to move in and repair the damage, followed by the electrician, the plasterer, the tile-layer, the carpenter and the painter. Since they were all good Provençaux, there was no chance at all that dates would be observed, but it provided the opportunity for some entertaining speculation.

Menicucci was enjoying his position of eminence as the key figure, the man whose progress would dictate the timetable of everyone else.

'You will see,' he said, 'that I have been obliged to make a Gorgonzola of the walls, but what is that, *maçon*? Half a day to repair?'

'Maybe a day,' said Didier. 'But when?'

'Don't try to rush me,' said Menicucci. 'Forty years as a plumber have taught me that you cannot hurry central heating. It is *très, très délicat.*'

'Christmas?' suggested Didier.

Menicucci looked at him, shaking his head. 'You joke about it, but think of the winter.' He demonstrated winter for us, wrapping an imaginary overcoat around his shoulders. 'It is minus ten degrees.' He shivered, pulling his bonnet over his ears. 'All of a sudden, the pipes start to leak! And why? Because they have been placed too quickly and without proper attention.' He looked at his audience, letting them appreciate the full drama of a cold and leaking winter. 'Who will be laughing then? Eh? Who will be making jokes about the plumber?'

It certainly wouldn't be me. The central heating experience so far had been a nightmare, made bearable only by the fact that we could stay outside during the day. Previous construction work had at least been confined to one part of the house, but this was everywhere. Menicucci and his copper tentacles were unavoidable. Dust and rubble and tortured fragments of piping marked his daily passage like the spoor of an iron-jawed termite. And, perhaps worst of all, there was no privacy. We were just as likely to find *jeune* in the bathroom with a blowlamp as to come across Menicucci's rear end sticking out of a hole in the living room wall. The pool was the only refuge, and even there it was best to be completely submerged so that the water muffled the relentless noise of drills and hammers. We sometimes thought that our friends were right, and that we should have gone away for August, or hidden in the deep freeze.

The evenings were such a relief that we usually stayed at home, convalescing after the din of the day, and so we missed most of the social and cultural events that had been organised for the benefit of summer visitors to the Lubéron. Apart from a bottom-numbing evening in the Abbey of Senanque, listening to Gregorian chants as we sat on benches of appropriately monastic discomfort, and a concert held in a floodlit ruin above Oppède, we didn't move from the courtyard. It was enough just to be alone and to be quiet.

Hunger eventually forced us out one night when we discovered that what we had planned to have for dinner had acquired a thick coating of grit from the day's drilling. We decided to go to a simple restaurant in Goult, a small village with an invisible population and no tourist attractions of any kind. It would be like eating at home, but cleaner. We beat a layer of dust from our clothes and left the dogs to guard the holes in the walls.

It had been a still, oppressively hot day, and the village smelt of heat, of baked tarmac and dried-out rosemary and warm gravel. And people. We had chosen the night of the annual fête.

We should have known, because every village celebrated August in one way or another – with a *boules* tournament or a donkey race or a barbecue or a fair, with coloured lights strung in the plane trees and dance floors made from wooden planks laid across scaffolding, with gypsies and accordion players and souvenir sellers and rock groups from as far away as Avignon. They were noisy, enjoyable occasions unless, like us, you were suffering from the mild concussion brought on by spending the day in a construction site. But we were there and we wanted the dinner that we had already mentally ordered. What were a few extra people compared to the delights of a salad made with warm mussels and bacon, chicken tickled with ginger and the chef's clinging and delicious chocolate cake?

At any other time of the year, the sight of more than a dozen people in the village streets would indicate an event of unusual interest – a funeral, perhaps, or a price-cutting war between the two butchers who had adjacent shops a few yards from the café. But this was an exceptional night; Goult was playing host to the world, and the world was obviously as hungry as we were. The restaurant was full. The terrace outside the restaurant was full. Hopeful couples lurked in the shadows under the trees, waiting for a free table. The waiters looked harassed. The proprietor, Patrick, looked tired but satisfied, a man with a temporary gold mine. 'You should have called,' he said. 'Come back at ten and I'll see what I can do.'

Even the café, which was large enough to hold the entire population of Goult, could offer standing room only. We took our drinks across the road, where stalls had been set up in a hollow square around the monument honouring the men of the village who had fought and died in the wars, fallen for the glory of France. Like most war memorials we had seen, it was respectfully well kept, with a cluster of three new *tricolore* flags sharp and clean against the grey stone.

The windows in the houses round the square were open and the occupants leant out, their flickering television sets forgotten behind them as they watched the slow-moving confusion below. It was more of a market than anything else, local artisans with their carved wood and pottery, wine-growers and honey-makers, a few antique dealers and artists. The heat of the day could be felt in the stone walls and seen in the way that the lazy, drifting crowd was walking, weight back on the heels, stomachs out, shoulders relaxed in a holiday slouch.

Most of the stands were trestle tables, with artefacts displayed on print tablecloths, often with a notice propped up saying that the owner could be found in the café if there was any risk of a sale. One stand, larger and more elaborate than the others, looked like an outdoor sitting room, furnished with tables and chairs and chaises longues and decorated with potted palms. A dark, stocky man in shorts and sandals sat at one of the tables with a bottle of wine and an order book. It was Monsieur Aude, the artist *ferronnier* of Saint-Pantaléon, who had done some work on the house. He beckoned us to sit down with him.

The *ferronnier* is a man who works with iron and steel, and in rural France he is kept busy making bars and gates and shutters and grilles to keep out the burglars who are assumed to be behind every bush. Monsieur Aude had progressed beyond these simple security devices, and had discovered that there was a market for replicas of classical eighteenth- and nineteenth-century steel furniture. He had a book of photographs and designs, and if you wanted a park bench or a baker's grill or a folding campaign bed such as Napoleon might have used, he would make it for you, then season it, being a superb judge of rust, to the required state of antiquity. He worked with his brother-in-law and a small beagle bitch and he could be relied upon to quote a delivery time of two weeks for anything, and to arrive with it three months later. We asked him if business was good.

He tapped his order book. 'I could open a factory – Germans, Parisians, Belgians. This year they all want the big round tables and these garden chairs.' He moved the chair next to him so that we could see the graceful arch of the legs. 'The problem is that they think I can make everything in a couple of days, and as you know . . .' he left the sentence unfinished, and chewed reflectively on a mouthful of wine. A couple who had been circling the stand came up and asked about a campaign bed. Monsieur Aude opened his book and licked the point of his pencil, then looked up at them. 'I have to tell you,' he said with a completely straight face, 'that it might take two weeks.'

It was almost eleven by the time we started to eat, and well past midnight when we got home. The air was warm and heavy and abnormally still. It was a night for the pool, and we slipped into the water to float on our backs and look at the stars – the perfect end to a sweltering day. A long way off, from the direction of the Côte d'Azur, there was a mutter of thunder and the brief flicker of lightning, distant and ornamental, somebody else's storm.

It reached Ménerbes in the dark and early hours of the morning, waking us with a clap that shook the windows and startled the dogs into a chorus of barking. For an hour or more it seemed to stay directly above the house, rolling and exploding and floodlighting the vineyard. And then it rained with the intensity of a burst dam, crashing on the roof and in the courtyard, dripping down the chimney and seeping under the front door. It stopped just after dawn and, as if nothing had happened, the sun came up as usual.

We had no electricity. A little later, when we tried to call the Electricité de France office, we found we had no 'phone line. When we walked round the house to see what the storm had destroyed we saw that half the drive had been washed into the road, leaving ruts as wide as tractor wheels and deep enough to be dangerous to any normal car. But there were two silver linings: it was a beautiful morning, and there were no workmen. They were undoubtedly too busy with their own leaks to worry about our central heating. We went for a walk in the forest, to see what the storm had done there.

It was dramatic, not because of any uprooted trees, but because of the effects of the deluge on earth that had been baked for weeks. Wraiths of steam rose among the trees, and with them a continuous hissing sound as the heat of the new day started to dry the undergrowth. We came back for a late breakfast filled with the optimism that sunshine and blue sky can inspire, and we were rewarded by a working 'phone, with Monsieur Fructus on the end of it. He had called to see if his insurance policy had suffered any damage.

We told him that the only casualty had been the drive.

'C'est bieng,' he said, 'I have a client who has fifty centimetres of water in his kitchen. It sometimes happens. August is bizarre.'

He was right. It had been a strange month, and we were glad it was over so that life could return to the way it had been before, with empty roads and uncrowded restaurants and Menicucci back in long trousers.

SEPTEMBER

Overnight, the population of the Lubéron dwindled. The *résidences secondaires* – some fine old houses among them – were locked and shuttered, their gateposts manacled with rusting lengths of chain. The houses would stay empty now until Christmas, so obviously, visibly empty that it was easy to understand why housebreaking in the Vaucluse had achieved the importance of a minor industry. Even the most poorly equipped and slow-moving of burglars could count on several undisturbed months in which to do his work, and in past years there had been some highly original thefts. Entire kitchens had been dismantled and taken away, old Roman roof tiles, an antique front door, a mature olive tree – it was as if a discerning burglar was setting up house with the choicest items he could find, selected with a connoisseur's eye from a variety of properties. Maybe he was the villain who had taken our mail box.

We began to see our local friends again as they emerged from the summer siege. Most of them were recovering from a surfeit of guests, and there was a certain awful similarity in the stories they told. Plumbing and money were the main topics, and it was astonishing how often the same phrases were used by mystified, apologetic or tight-fisted visitors. Unwittingly, they had compiled between them The Sayings of August.

'What do you mean, they don't take credit cards? Everyone takes credit cards.'

'You've run out of vodka.'

'There's a very peculiar smell in the bathroom.'

'Do you think you could take care of this? I've only got a 500-franc note.'

'Don't worry. I'll send you a replacement as soon as I get back to London.'

'I didn't realise you had to be so careful with a septic tank.'

'Don't forget to let me know how much those calls to Los Angeles were.'

'I feel terrible watching you slave away like that.'

'You've run out of whisky.'

As we listened to the tales of blocked drains and guzzled brandy, of broken wine glasses in the swimming pool, of sealed wallets and prodigious appetites, we felt that we had been very kindly treated during August. Our house had suffered considerable damage, but from the sound of it our friends' houses had suffered too. At least we hadn't had to provide food and lodging for Menicucci while he was wreaking havoc.

In many ways, the early part of September felt like a second spring. The days were dry and hot, the nights cool, the air wonderfully clear after the muggy haze of August. The inhabitants of the valley had shaken off their torpor and were getting down to the main business of the year, patrolling their vineyards every morning to examine the grapes that hung for mile after mile in juicy and orderly lines.

Faustin was out there with the rest of them, cupping the bunches in his hand and looking up at the sky, sucking his teeth in contemplation as he tried to second guess the weather. I asked him when he thought he was going to pick.

'They should cook some more,' he said. 'But the weather in September is not to be trusted.'

He had made the same gloomy comment about the weather every month of the year so far, in the resigned and plaintive tones used by farmers all over the world when they tell you how hard it is to scratch a living from the land. Conditions are never right. The rain, the wind, the sunshine, the weeds, the insects, the government – there is always at least one fly in their ointment, and they take a perverse pleasure in their pessimism.

'You can do everything right for eleven months a year,' said Faustin, 'and then – *pouf* – a storm comes and the crop is hardly fit for grape juice.' *Jus de raiseng* – he said it with such scorn that I could imagine him leaving a spoilt crop to rot on the vines rather than waste his time picking grapes that couldn't even aspire to become *vin ordinaire*.

As if his life were not already filled with grief, nature had put a further difficulty in his way: the grapes on our land would have to be picked at two separate times, because about five hundred of our vines produced table grapes which would be ready before the *raisins de cuve*. This was *un emmerdement*, made tolerable only because of the good price that table grapes fetched. Even so, it meant that there were two possible occasions when disappointment and disaster could strike and, if Faustin knew anything about it, strike they undoubtedly would. I left him shaking his head and grumbling to God.

To make up for the mournful predictions of Faustin, we received a daily ration of joyful news from Menicucci, now coming to the end of his labours on the central heating system and almost beside himself with anticipation as the day of firing up the boiler approached. Three times he reminded me to order the oil, and then insisted on supervising the filling of the tank to make sure that the delivery was free from foreign bodies.

'*Il faut très attention*,' he explained to the man who brought the oil. 'The smallest piece of *cochonnerie* in your fuel will affect my burner and clog the electrodes. I think it would be prudent to filter it as you pump it into the tank.'

The fuel man drew himself up in outrage, parrying Menicucci's wagging finger with his own, oily and black-rimmed at the tip. 'My fuel is already triple-filtered. *C'est impeccable*.' He made as if to kiss his fingertips and then thought better of it.

'We shall see,' said Menicucci. 'We shall see.' He looked with suspicion at the nozzle before it was placed inside the tank, and the fuel man wiped it ostentatiously on a filthy rag. The filling ceremony was accompanied by a detailed technical discourse on the inner workings of the burner and the boiler which the fuel man listened to with scant interest, grunting or saying *Ah bon?* whenever his participation was required. Menicucci turned to me as the last few litres were pumped in. 'This afternoon we will have the first test.' He had an anxious moment as a dreadful possibility occurred to him. 'You're not going out? You and Madame will be here?' It would have been an act of supreme unkindness to deprive him of his audience. We promised to be ready and waiting at two o'clock.

We gathered in what had once been a dormitory for donkeys, now transformed by Menicucci into the nerve centre of his heating complex. Boiler, burner and water tank were arranged side by side, joined together by umbilical cords of copper, and an impressive array of painted pipes – red for hot water, blue for cold, *très logique* – fanned out from the boiler and disappeared into the ceiling. Valves and dials and switches, bright and incongruous against the rough stone of the walls, awaited the master's touch. It looked extremely complicated, and I made the mistake of saying so.

Menicucci took it as a personal criticism, and spent ten minutes demonstrating its astonishing simplicity, flicking switches, opening and closing valves, twiddling dials and gauges and making me thoroughly bewildered. '*Voilà!*' he said after a final flourish on the switches. 'Now that you understand the apparatus, we will start the test. *Jeune!* Pay attention.'

The beast awoke with a series of clicks and snuffles. '*Le brûleur,*' said Menicucci, dancing round the boiler to adjust the controls for the fifth time. There was a thump of air, and then a muffled roar. 'We have combustion!' He made it sound as dramatic as the launch of a space shuttle. 'Within five minutes, every radiator will be hot. Come!'

He scuttled round the house, insisting that we touch each radiator. 'You see? You will be able to pass the entire winter *en chemise.*' By this time, we were all sweating profusely. It was eighty degrees outside, and the indoor temperature with the heating full on was insufferable. I asked if we could turn it off before we dehydrated.

'*Ah non.* You must leave it on for twenty-four hours so that we can verify all the joins and make sure there are no leaks. Touch nothing until I return tomorrow. It is most important that everything remains at maximum.' He left us to wilt, and to enjoy the smell of cooked dust and hot iron.

* * * * *

There is one September weekend when the countryside sounds as though rehearsals are being held for World War Three. It is the official start of the hunting season, and every red-blooded Frenchman takes his gun, his dog and his murderous inclinations into the hills in search of sport. The first sign that this was about to happen came through the post – a terrifying document from a gunsmith in Vaison-la-Romaine, offering a complete range of artillery at pre-season prices. There were sixty or seventy models to choose from, and my hunting instincts, which had been dormant since birth, were aroused by the thought of owning a Verney Carron Grand Bécassier, or a Ruger ·44 Magnum with an electronic sight. My wife, who has a well-founded lack of confidence in my ability to handle any kind of dangerous equipment, pointed out that I hardly needed an electronic sight to shoot myself in the foot.

We had both been surprised at the French fondness for guns. Twice we had visited the homes of outwardly mild and unwarlike men, and twice we had been shown the family arsenal; one man had five rifles of various calibres, the other had eight, oiled and polished and displayed in a rack on the dining room wall like a lethal piece of art. How could anyone need eight guns? How would you know which one to take with you? or did you take them all, like a bag of golf clubs, selecting the ·44 Magnum for leopard or moose and the Baby Bretton for rabbit?

After a while, we came to realise that the gun mania was only part of a national fascination with outfits and accoutrements, a passion for looking like an expert. When a Frenchman takes up cycling or tennis or skiing, the last thing he wants is for the world to mistake him for the novice that he is, and so he accessorises himself up to professional standard. It's instant. A few thousand francs and there you are, indistinguishable from any other seasoned ace competing in the Tour de France or Wimbledon or the Winter Olympics. In the case of *la chasse*, the accessories are almost limitless, and they have the added attraction of being deeply masculine and dangerous in their appearance.

We were treated to a preview of hunting fashions in Cavaillon market. The stalls had stocked up for the season, and looked like small paramilitary depots: there were cartridge bandoliers and plaited leather rifle slings; jerkins with myriad zippered pockets and game pouches that were washable and therefore *très pratique*, because bloodstains could be easily removed; there were wilderness boots of the kind used by mercenaries parachuting into the Congo; fearsome knives with nine-inch blades and compasses set into the handle; lightweight aluminium water bottles which would probably see more pastis than water; webbing belts with D-rings and a special sling to hold a bayonet, presumably in case the ammunition ran out and game had to be attacked with cold steel; forage caps and commando trousers, survival rations and tiny collapsible field stoves. There was everything a man might need for his confrontation with the untamed beasts of the forest except that indispensable accessory with four legs and a nose like radar, the hunting dog.

Chiens de chasse are too specialised to be bought and sold across a counter, and we were told that no serious hunter would consider buying a pup without first meeting both parents. Judging by some of the hunting dogs we had seen, we could imagine that finding the father might have been difficult, but among all the hybrid curiosities there were three more or less identifiable types – the liver-coloured approximation of a large spaniel, the stretched beagle, and the tall, rail-thin hound with the wrinkled, lugubrious face.

Every hunter considers his dog to be uniquely gifted, and he will have at least one implausible story of stamina and prowess to tell you. To hear the owners talk, you would think that these dogs were supernaturally intelligent creatures, trained to a hair and faithful unto death. We looked forward with interest to seeing them perform on the opening weekend of the season. Perhaps their example would inspire our dogs to do something more useful than stalk lizards and attack old tennis balls.

Hunting in our part of the valley started shortly after seven o'clock one Sunday morning, with salvoes coming from either side of the house and from the mountains behind. It sounded as though anything that moved would be at risk, and when I went out for a walk with the dogs I took the biggest white handkerchief I could find in case I needed to surrender. With infinite caution, we set off along the footpath that runs behind the house towards the village, assuming that any hunter worth his gun licence would have moved well away from the beaten track and into the tangled undergrowth further up the mountain.

There was a noticeable absence of birdsong; all sensible or experienced birds had left at the sound of the first shot for somewhere safer, like North Africa or central Avignon. In the bad old days, hunters used to hang caged birds in the trees to lure other birds close enough for a point-blank shot, but that had been made illegal, and the modern hunter now had to rely on woodcraft and stealth.

I didn't see much evidence of that, but I did see enough hunters and dogs and weaponry to wipe out the entire thrush and rabbit population of southern France. They hadn't gone up into the forest; in fact, they had barely left the footpath. Knots of them were gathered in the clearings – laughing, smoking, taking nips from their khaki-painted flasks and cutting slices of *saucisson*, but of active hunting – man versus thrush in a battle of wits – there was no sign. They must have used up their ration of shells during the early morning fusillade.

Their dogs, however, were anxious to get to work. After months of confinement in kennels, they were delirious with liberty and the scents of the forest, tracking back and forth, noses close to the ground and twitching with excitement. Each dog wore a thick collar with a small brass bell – the *clochette* – hanging from it. We were told that this had a double purpose. It signalled the dog's whereabouts so that the hunter could position himself for the game that was being driven towards him, but it was also a precaution against shooting at something in the bushes that sounded like a rabbit or a boar and finding that you had shot your own dog. No responsible hunter, *naturellement*, would ever shoot at anything he couldn't see – or so I was told. But I had my doubts. After a morning with the pastis or the *marc*, a rustle in the bushes might be too much to resist, and the cause of the rustle might be human. In fact, it might be me. I thought about wearing a bell, just to be on the safe side.

Another benefit of the *clochette* became apparent at the end of the morning: it was to help the hunter avoid the humiliating experience of losing his dog at the end of the hunt. Far from the disciplined and faithful animals I had imagined them to be, hunting dogs are wanderers, led on by their noses and oblivious to the passage of time. They have not grasped the idea that hunting stops for lunch. The bell doesn't necessarily mean that the dog will come when called, but at least the hunter can tell roughly where he is.

Just before noon, camouflage-clad figures started to make their way to the vans parked at the side of the road. A few had dogs with them. The rest were whistling and shouting with increasing irritation, making a bad-tempered hissing noise – '*Vieng ici!*' *Vieng ici!*' – in the direction of the symphony of bells that could be heard coming from the forest.

Response was patchy. The shouts became more bad-tempered, degenerating into bellows and curses. After a few minutes the hunters gave up and went home, most of them dogless.

We were joined a little later for lunch by three abandoned hounds who came down to drink the swimming pool. They were greatly admired by our two bitches for their devil-may-care manner and exotic aroma, and we penned them all in the courtyard while we wondered how we could get them back to their owners. We consulted Faustin.

'Don't bother,' he said. 'Let them go. The hunters will be back in the evening. If they don't find their dogs, they'll leave a *coussin*.'

It always worked, so Faustin said. If the dog was in the forest, one simply left something with the scent of the kennel on it – a cushion or, more likely, a scrap of sacking – near the spot where the dog had last been seen. Sooner or later, the dog would come back to its own scent and wait to be picked up.

We let the three hounds out, and they loped off, baying with excitement. It was an extraordinary, doleful sound, not a bark or a howl but a lament, like an oboe in pain. Faustin shook his head. 'They'll be gone for days.' He himself didn't hunt, and regarded hunters and their dogs as intruders who had no right to be nosing around his precious vines.

He had decided, he told us, that the moment had come to pick the table grapes. They would start as soon as Henriette had finished servicing the *camion*. She was the mechanically minded member of the family, and every September she had the job of coaxing another few kilometres out of the grape truck. It was at least thirty years old – maybe more, Faustin couldn't remember exactly – blunt-nosed and rickety, with open sides and bald tyres. It had ceased to be roadworthy years ago, but there was no question of buying a new truck. And why waste good money having it serviced at a garage when you had a mechanic for a wife? It was only used for a few weeks a year, and Faustin was careful to take it on the back roads to avoid meeting any of those officious little *flics* from the police station at Les Baumettes, with their absurd regulations about brakes and valid insurance.

Henriette's ministrations were successful, and the old truck gasped up the drive early one morning, loaded with shallow wooden grape trays, just deep enough for a single layer of bunches. Stacks of trays were placed along each line of vines, and the three of them – Faustin, Henriette and their daughter – took their scissors and set to work.

It was a slow and physically uncomfortable business. Because the appearance of table grapes is almost as important as their taste, every bunch had to be examined, every bruised or wrinkled grape snipped off. The bunches grew low, sometimes touching the earth and hidden by leaves, and the pickers' progress was in yards per hour – squatting down, cutting, standing up, inspecting, snipping, packing. The heat was fierce, coming up from the ground as well as beating down on the necks and shoulders. No shade, no breeze, no relief in the course of a ten-hour day except the break for lunch. Never again would I look at a bunch of grapes in a bowl without thinking of backache and sunstroke. It was past seven when they came in for a drink, exhausted and radiating heat, but satisfied. The grapes were good and three or four days would see them all picked. I said to Faustin that he must be pleased with the weather. He pushed back his hat and I could see the line sharp across his forehead where the burnt brown skin turned white.

'It's too good,' he said. 'It won't last.' He took a long pull at his pastis as he considered the spectrum of misfortunes that could occur. If not storms, there might be a freak frost, a plague of locusts, a forest fire, a nuclear attack. Something was bound to go wrong before the second batch of grapes was picked. And, if it didn't, he could console himself with the fact that his doctor had put him on a diet to reduce his cholesterol level. Yes, that was certainly a grave problem. Reassured at having remembered that fate had recently dealt him a black card, he had another drink.

* * * * *

It had taken me some time to get used to having a separate, purpose-built room devoted exclusively to wine – not a glorified cupboard or a cramped cavity under the stairs, but a genuine *cave*. It was buried in the bottom of the house, with permanently cool stone walls and a floor of gravel, and there was space for three or four hundred bottles. I loved it. I was determined to fill it up. Our friends were equally determined to empty it. This gave me the excuse to make regular visits – errands of social mercy – to the vineyards so that guests should never go thirsty.

In the interests of research and hospitality, I went to Gigondas and Beaumes-de-Venise and Châteauneuf-du-Pape, none of them bigger than a large village, all of them single-minded in their dedication to the grape. Everywhere I looked, there were signs advertising the *caves* that seemed to be at fifty-yard intervals. *Dégustez nos vins*! Never has a invitation been accepted with more enthusiasm. I had *dégustations* in a garage in Gigondas and a château above Beaumes-de-Venise. I found a powerful and velvety Châteauneuf-du-Pape for 30 francs a litre, squirted into plastic containers with a marvellous lack of ceremony from what looked like a garage pump. In a more expensive and more pretentious establishment, I asked to try the *marc*. A small cut-glass bottle was produced, and a drop was dabbed on the back of my hand, whether to sniff or to suck I wasn't quite sure.

After a while, I bypassed the villages and started to follow the signs, often half hidden by vegetation, that pointed deep into the countryside where the wines baked in the sun, and where I could buy direct from the men who made the wine. They were, without exception, hospitable and proud of their work and, to me at least, their sales pitch was irresistible.

It was early afternoon when I turned off the main road leading out of Vacqueyras and followed the narrow, stony track through the vines. I had been told that it would lead me to the maker of the wine I had liked at lunchtime, a white Côtes-du-Rhône. A case or two would fill the void in the *cave* that had been made by the last raiding party we had entertained. A quick stop, no more than ten minutes, and then I would get back home.

The track led to a sprawl of buildings, arranged in a square U around a courtyard of beaten earth, shaded by a giant plane tree and guarded by a drowsy Alsatian who welcomed me with a half-hearted bark, doing his duty as a substitute for a doorbell. A man in overalls, holding an oily collection of spark plugs, came over from his tractor. He gave me his forearm to shake.

I wanted some white wine? Of course. He himself was busy nursing his tractor, but his uncle would take care of me. '*Edouard! Tu peux servir ce monsieur?*'

The curtain of wooden beads hanging across the front door parted, and Uncle Edward came blinking into the sunshine. He was wearing a sleeveless vest, cotton *bleu de travail* trousers and carpet slippers. His girth was impressive, comparable with with trunk of the plane tree, but even that was overshadowed by his nose. I had never seen a nose quite like it – wide, fleshy and seasoned to a colour somewhere between rosé and claret, with fine purple lines spreading out across his cheeks. Here was a man who clearly enjoyed every mouthful of his work.

He beamed, the lines on his cheeks looking like purple whiskers. '*Bon. Une petite dégustation.*' He led me across the courtyard and slid back the double doors of a long, windowless building, telling me to stay just inside the door while he went to switch on the light. After the glare outside, I could see nothing, but there was a reassuring smell, musty and unmistakable, the air itself tasting of fermented grapes.

Uncle Edward turned on the light and closed the doors against the heat. A long trestle table and half a dozen chairs were placed under the single light bulb with its flat tin shade. In a dark corner, I could make out a flight of stairs and a concrete ramp leading down into the cellar. Crates of wine were stacked on wooden pallets around the walls, and an old refrigerator hummed quietly next to a cracked sink.

Uncle Edward was polishing glasses, holding each one up to the light before placing it on the table. He made a neat line of seven glasses, and began to arrange a variety of bottles behind them. Each bottle was accorded a few admiring comments: 'The white monsieur knows, yes? A very agreeable young wine. The rosé, not at all like those thin rosés one finds on the Côte d'Azur. Thirteen degrees of alcohol, a proper wine. There's a light red – one could drink a bottle of that before a game of tennis. That one, *par contre*, is for the winter, and he will keep for ten years or more. And then . . .'

I tried to stop him. I told him that all I wanted were two cases of the white, but he wouldn't hear of it. Monsieur had taken the trouble to come personally, and it would be unthinkable not to taste a selection. Why, said Uncle Edward, he himself would join me in a progress through the vintages. He clapped a heavy hand on my shoulder and sat me down.

It was fascinating. He told me the precise part of the vineyard that each of the wines had come from, and why certain slopes produced lighter or heavier wines. Each wine we tasted was accompanied by an imaginary menu, described with much lip-smacking and raising of the eyes to gastronomic heaven. We mentally consumed *écrevisses*, salmon cooked with sorrel, rosemary-flavoured chicken from Bresse, roasted baby lamb with a creamy garlic sauce, an *estouffade* of beef and olives, a *daube*, loin of pork spiked with slivers of truffle. The wines tasted progressively better and became progressively more expensive; I was being traded up by an expert, and there was nothing to be done except sit back and enjoy it.

'There is one more you should try,' said Uncle Edward, 'although it is not to everybody's taste.' He picked up a bottle and poured a careful half glass. It was deep red, almost black. 'A wine of great character,' he said. 'Wait. It needs *une bonne bouche*.' He left me surrounded by glasses and bottles, feeling the first twinges of an afternoon hangover.

'*Voilà.*' He put a plate in front of me – two small round goats' cheeses, speckled with herbs and shiny with oil – and gave me a knife with a worn wooden handle. He watched as I cut off a piece of cheese and ate it. It was ferociously strong. My palate, or what was left of it, had been perfectly primed and the wine tasted like nectar.

Uncle Edward helped me load the cases into the car. Had I really ordered all this? I must have done. We had been sitting in the convivial murk for nearly two hours, and one can make all kinds of expansive decisions in two hours. I left with a throbbing head and an invitation to come back next month for the *vendange*.

Our own *vendange*, the agricultural highlight of the year, took place during the last week of September. Faustin would have liked it to be a few day later, but he had some private information about the weather which convinced him that it would be a wet October.

The original party of three that had picked the table grapes was reinforced by Cousin Raoul and Faustin's father. His contribution was to walk slowly behind the pickers, prodding among the vines with his stick until he found a bunch of grapes that had been overlooked and then shouting – he had a good, carrying bellow for a man of eighty-four – for someone to come back and do the job properly. In contrast to the others in their shorts and vests, he was dressed for a brisk November day in a sweater, a cap and a suit of heavy cotton. When my wife appeared with a camera, he took off his cap, smoothed his hair, put his cap back on and struck a pose, waist-deep in vines. Like all our neighbours, he loved having his portrait taken.

Slowly and noisily, the rows were picked clean, the grapes piled into plastic crates and stacked in the back of the truck. Every evening now, the roads were busy with vans and tractors towing their purple mountains to the wine co-operative at Maubec, where they were weighed and tested for alcoholic content.

To Faustin's surprise, the crop was gathered without incident, and to celebrate he invited us to go with him to the co-operative when he made the last delivery. 'Tonight we will see the final figures,' he said, 'and then you will know how much you can drink next year.'

We followed the truck as it swayed off into the sunset at twenty

miles an hour, keeping to narrow roads that were stained with fallen, squashed grapes. There was a queue waiting to unload. Burly men with roasted faces sat on their tractors until it was their turn to back up to the platform and tip their loads down the chute – the first stage of their journey to the bottle.

Faustin finished unloading, and we went with him into the building to see our grapes going into the huge stainless steel vats. 'Watch that dial,' he said. 'It shows the degrees of alcohol.' The needle swung up, quivered and settled at 12·32 per cent. Faustin grunted. He would have liked 12·50 and an extra few days in the sun might have done it, but anything above 12 was reasonable. He took us over to the man who kept the tallies of each delivery and peered at a line of figures on a clipboard, matching them with a handful of slips of paper he pulled from his pocket. He nodded. It was all correct.

'You won't go thirsty.' He made the Provençal drinking gesture, fist clenched and thumb pointing towards his mouth. 'Just over one thousand two hundred litres.'

It sounded like a good year to us, and we told Faustin we were pleased. 'Well,' he said, 'at least it didn't rain.'

* * * * *

OCTOBER

The man stood peering into the moss and light undergrowth around the roots of an old scrub oak tree. His right leg was encased up to the thigh in a green rubber fishing wader; on the other foot was a running shoe. He held a long stick in front of him and carried a blue plastic shopping basket.

He turned sideways on to the tree, advanced the rubber-clad leg and plunged his stick nervously into the vegetation, in the manner of a fencer expecting a sudden and violent riposte. And again, with the rubber leg pushed forward: on guard, thrust, withdraw, thrust. He was so absorbed by his duel that he had no idea that I was watching, equally absorbed, from the path. One of the dogs went up behind him and gave his rear leg an exploratory sniff.

He jumped – *merde!* – and then saw the dog, and me, and looked embarrassed. I apologised for startling him.

'For a moment,' he said, 'I thought I was being attacked.'

I couldn't imagine who he thought was going to sniff his leg before attacking him, and I asked what he was looking for. In reply, he held up his shopping basket. *'Les champignons.'*

This was a new and worrying aspect of the Lubéron. It was, as I already knew, a region full of strange things and even stranger people. But surely mushrooms, even wild mushrooms, didn't attack fully grown men. I asked him if the mushrooms were dangerous.

'Some can kill you,' he said.

That I could believe, but it didn't explain the rubber boot or the extraordinary performance with the stick. At the risk of being made to feel like the most ignorant of city-reared dunces, I pointed at his right leg.

'The boot is for protection?'

'*Mais oui.*'

'But against what?'

He slapped the rubber with his wooden sword and swaggered down towards me, D'Artagnan with a shopping basket. He delivered a backhand cut at a clump of thyme and came closer.

'*Les serpents.*' He said it with just the trace of a hiss. 'They are preparing for winter. If you disturb them – sssst! – they attack. It can be very grave.'

He showed me the contents of his shopping basket, snatched from the forest at the risk of life and limb. To me, they looked highly poisonous, varying in colour from blue-black to rust to violent orange, not at all like the civilised white mushrooms sold in the markets. He held the basket under my nose, and I breathed in what he called the essence of the mountains. To my surprise, it was good – earthy, rich, slightly nutty – and I looked at the mushrooms more closely. I had seen them in the forest, in evil-looking clusters under the trees, and had assumed that they were instant death. My booted friend assured me that they were not only safe, but delicious.

'But,' he said, 'you must know the deadly species. There are two or three. If you're not sure, take them to the pharmacy.'

It had never occurred to me that a mushroom could be clinically tested before being permitted to enter an omelette but, since the stomach is by far the most influential organ in France, it made perfect sense. The next time I went into Cavaillon, I toured the pharmacies. Sure enough, they had been converted into mushroom guidance centres. The window displays, normally devoted to surgical trusses and pictures of young women reducing the cellulite on their slim bronzed thighs, now featured large mushroom identification charts. Some pharmacies went even further, and filled their windows with piles of reference books which described and illustrated every species of edible fungus known to man.

I saw people going into the pharmacies with grubby bags which they presented at the counter rather anxiously, as though they were undergoing tests for a rare disease. The small, muddy objects in the bags were solemnly inspected by the resident white-coated expert, and a verdict was pronounced. I suppose it made an interesting change from the usual daily round of suppositories and liver tonics. I found it so distracting that I almost forgot why I had come to Cavaillon – not to loiter around pharmacies but to shop for bread at the local shrine of baking.

Living in France had turned us into bakery addicts, and the business of choosing and buying our daily bread was a recurring pleasure. The village bakery in Ménerbes, with its erratic opening hours – 'Madame will re-open when she has finished making her *toilette*,' I was told one day – had first encouraged us to visit other bakeries in other villages. It was a revelation. After years of taking bread for granted, more or less as a standard commodity, it was like discovering a new food.

We tried the dense, chewy loaves from Lumières, fatter and flatter than the ordinary *baguette*, and the dark-crusted *boules*, as big as squashed footballs, from Cabrières. We learned which breads would keep for a day, and which would be stale in three hours; the best bread for making *croûtons* or for spreading with *rouille* to launch into a sea of fish soup. We became used to the delightful but initially surprising sight of bottles of champagne offered for sale next to the tarts and tiny individual pastries that were made fresh every morning and gone by noon.

Most of the bakeries had their own touches which distinguished their loaves from mass-produced supermarket bread: slight variations from conventional shapes, an extra whorl of crusty decoration, an elaborate pattern, the artist baker signing his work. It was as if the sliced, wrapped, machine-made loaf had never been invented.

In Cavaillon, there are seventeen bakers listed in the *Pages Jaunes*, but we had been told that one establishment was ahead of all the rest in terms of choice and excellence, a veritable *palais de pain*. At Chez Auzet, so they said, the baking and eating of breads

and pastries had been elevated to the status of a minor religion.

When the weather is warm, tables and chairs are placed on the pavement outside the bakery so that the matrons of Cavaillon can sit with their hot chocolate and almond biscuits or strawberry tarts while they give proper, leisurely consideration to the bread they will buy for lunch and dinner. To help them, Auzet has printed a comprehensive bread menu; the *Carte des Pains*. I took a copy from the counter, ordered coffee, sat in the sun and started to read.

It was another step in my French education. Not only did it introduce me to breads I had never heard of before, it told me with great firmness and precision what I should be eating with them. With my *apéritif*, I could choose between the tiny squares called *toasts*, a *pain surprise* which might be flavoured with finely chopped bacon, or the savoury *feuillets salés*, That was simple. The decisions became more complicated when the meal itself was being chosen. Supposing, for example, I wanted to start with *crudités*. There were four possible accompaniments: onion bread, garlic bread, olive bread or roquefort bread. Too difficult? In that case, I could have seafood, because the gospel according the Auzet authorised only one bread to eat with seafood, and that was thinly-sliced rye.

And so it went on, listing with uncompromising brevity what I should eat with *charcuterie*, foie gras, soup, red and white meat, game with feathers and game with fur, smoked meats, mixed salads (not to be confused with the separately listed green salads) and three different consistencies of cheese. I counted eighteen varieties of bread, from thyme to pepper, from nuts to bran. In a fog of indecision, I went inside the shop and consulted Madame. What would she recommend with calves' liver?

She set off on a short tour of the shelves, and then selected a stubby brown *banette*. While she was counting out my change, she told me about a restaurant where the chef serves a different bread with each of the five courses on his menu. There's a man who understands bread, she said. Not like some.

I was beginning to understand it, just as I was beginning to understand mushrooms. It had been an instructive morning.

* * * * *

Massot was in lyrical mood. He had just left his house to go into the forest and kill something when I met him on a hill overlooking a long stretch of vineyards. With his gun under his arm and one of his yellow cigarettes screwed into the corner of his mouth, he stood contemplating the valley.

'Look at those vines,' he said. 'Nature is wearing her prettiest clothes.'

The effect of this unexpectedly poetic observation was slightly spoiled when Massot cleared his throat noisily and spat, but he was right; the vines were spectacular, field after field of russet and yellow and scarlet leaves, motionless in the sunlight. Now that the grapes had all been picked there were no tractors or human figures to interfere with our appreciation of the view. Work on the vines wouldn't start again until the leaves had fallen and the pruning began. It was a space between seasons, still hot, but not quite summer and not yet autumn.

I asked Massot if there had been any progress in the sale of his property, maybe a nice German couple who had fallen in love with the house while camping nearby.

He bristled at the mention of campers. 'They couldn't afford a house like mine. In any case, I have taken it off the market until 1992. You'll see. When the frontiers are abolished, they'll all be looking for houses down here – English, Belgians . . .' He waved his hand airily to include the other Common Market nationalities. 'Prices will become much more important. Houses in the Lubéron will be *très recherchées*. Even your little place might fetch a million or two.'

It was not the first time that 1992 had been mentioned as the year when the whole of Provence would be showered with foreign money, because in 1992 the Common Market would come into its own. Nationalities would be forgotten as we all became one big happy family of Europeans. Financial restrictions would be lifted – and what would the Spaniards and Italians and the rest of them do? What else but hurry down to Provence waving their cheque books and looking for houses.

It was a popular thought, but I couldn't see why it should happen. Provence already had a considerable foreign population; they had found no problem buying houses. And, for all the talk of

European integration, a date on a piece of paper wasn't going to stop the bickering and bureaucracy and jockeying for special preference which all the member countries – notably France – used when it suited them. Fifty years might see a difference; 1992 almost certainly would not.

But Massot was convinced. In 1992, he was going to sell up and retire, or possibly buy a little *bar-tabac* in Cavaillon. I asked him what he'd do with his three dangerous dogs, and for a moment I thought he was going to burst into tears.

'They wouldn't be happy in a town,' he said. 'I'd have to shoot them.'

He walked along with me for a few minutes, and cheered himself up by muttering about the profits that were certain to come his way, and about time too. A lifetime of hard work should be rewarded. A man should spend his old age in comfort, not breaking his back on the land. As it happened, his land was exceptional in the valley for its ill-kempt appearance, but he always spoke of it as though it were a cross between the gardens at Villandry and the manicured vineyards of Château Lafite. He turned off the path to go into the forest and terrorise some birds, a brutal, greedy and mendacious old scoundrel. I was becoming quite fond of him.

The way home was littered with spent shotgun cartridges fired by the men whom Massot dismissed as *chasseurs du sentier*, or footpath hunters – miserable namby-pambies who didn't want to get their boots dirty in the forest, and who hoped that birds would somehow fly into their buckshot. Among the scattered shell cases were crushed cigarette packets and empty sardine cans and bottles, souvenirs left by the same nature lovers who complained that the beauty of the Lubéron was being ruined by tourists. Their concern for conservation didn't extend to removing their own rubbish. A messy breed, the Provençal hunter.

I arrived at the house to find a small conference taking place around the electricity meter which was hidden behind some trees in the back garden. The man from Electricité de France had opened the meter to read it, and had discovered that a colony of ants had made a nest. The figures were obscured. It was impossible to establish our consumption of electricity. The ants must be removed. My wife and the man from the EDF had been joined by Menicucci, whom we now suspected of living in the boiler room, and who liked nothing better than to advise us on any domestic problem that might arise.

'*Oh là là.*' A pause while Menicucci bent down for a closer look at the meter. '*Ils sont nombreux, les fourmis.*' For once, he had made an understatement. The ants were so numerous that they appeared as one solid black block, completely filling the metal box that housed the meter.

'I'm not touching them,' said the EDF man. 'They get into your clothes and bite you. The last time I tried to brush away an ants' nest I had them with me all afternoon.'

He stood looking at the squirming mass, tapping his screwdriver againt his teeth. He turned to Menicucci. 'Do you have a blowlamp?'

'I'm a plumber. Of course I have a blowlamp.'

'*Bon.* Then we can burn them off.'

Menicucci was aghast. He took a step backwards and crossed himself. He smote his forehead. He raised his index finger to the position that indicated either extreme disagreement, or the start of a lecture, or both.

'I cannot believe what I have just heard. A blowlamp? Do you realise how much current passes through here?'

The EDF man looked offended. 'Of course I know. I'm an electrician.'

Menicucci affected to be surprised. '*Ah bon?* Then you will know what happens when you burn a live cable.'

'I would be very prudent with the flame.'

'Prudent! Prudent! *Mon Dieu*, we could all perish with the ants.'

The EDF man sheathed his screwdriver and crossed his arms. 'Very well. I will not occupy myself with the ants. You remove them.'

Menicucci thought for a moment and then, like a magician setting up a particularly astonishing trick, he turned to my wife. 'If Madame could possibly bring me some fresh lemons – two or three will be enough – and a knife?'

Madame the magician's assistant came back with the knife and lemons, and Menicucci cut each into four quarters. 'This is an *astuce* that I was taught by a very old man,' he said, and muttered something impolite about the stupidity of using a blowlamp – '*putain de chalumeau*' – while the EDF man sulked under a tree.

When the lemons were all quartered, Menicucci advanced on the nest and started to squeeze lemon juice back and forth over the ants, pausing between squeezes to observe the effect that the downpour of citric acid was having.

The ants surrendered, evacuating the meter box in panic-stricken clumps, climbing over each other in their haste to escape. Menicucci enjoyed his moment of triumph. '*Voilà, jeune homme*,' he said to the EDF man, 'ants cannot support the juice of fresh lemons. That is something you have learned today. If you leave slices of lemon in your meters you will never have another infestation.'

The EDF man took it with a marked lack of graciousness, complaining that he was not a lemon-supplier and that the juice had made the meter sticky. 'Better sticky than burnt to a cinder,' was Menicucci's parting shot as he returned to his boiler. '*Beh oui.* Better sticky than burnt.'

* * * * *

The days were warm enough for swimming, the nights cool enough for fires, Indian summer weather. It finally ended in the excessive style that was typical of the Provençal climate. We went to bed in one season and woke up in another.

The rain had come in the night, and continued for most of the following day; not the fat, warm drops of summer, but grey sheets that fell in a vertical torrent, sluicing through the vineyards, flattening shrubs, turning flower beds into mud and mud into brown rivers. It stopped in the late afternoon, and we went to look at the drive – or, rather, where the drive had been the previous day.

It had already suffered in the big storm of August, but the ruts made then were scratches compared to what we now saw: a succession of craters led down to the road, where most of the drive had been deposited in sodden piles. The rest of it was in the melon field opposite the house. Some of the gravel and stones had travelled more than a hundred yards. A recently detonated mine-field could hardly have looked worse, and nobody except a man who hated his car would have attempted to drive to the house from the road. We needed a bulldozer just to tidy up the mess, and several tons of gravel to replace what the rain had washed away.

I called Monsieur Menicucci. Over the months, he had established himself as a human version of the Yellow Pages, and, since he had a regard verging on the proprietorial for our house, his recommendations had been made, so he told us, as though it were his own money at stake. He listened as I told him of the lost drive, making interjections – *quelle catastrophe* was mentioned more than once – to show that he appreciated the extent of the problem.

I finished talking, and I could hear Menicucci making a verbal list of our requirements: '*Un bulldozer, bien sûr, un camion, une montagne de gravier, un compacteur . . .*' There were a few moments of humming, probably a snatch of Mozart to assist the mental processes, and then he made up his mind.'*Bon.* There is a young man, the son of a neighbour, who is an artist with the bulldozer, and his prices are correct. He's called Sanchez. I will ask him to come tomorrow.'

I reminded Menicucci that the drive was not possible for an ordinary car.

'He's used to that,' said Menicucci. 'He will come on his *moto* with special tyres. He can pass anywhere.'

I watched him negotiate the drive the next morning, doing slalom turns to avoid the craters and standing up on his footrests as he drove over the mounds of earth. He cut the engine and looked back at the drive, a study in colour co-ordinated *moto chic*. His hair was black, his leather jacket was black, his bike was black. He wore aviator sunglasses with impenetrable reflective lenses. I wondered if he knew our insurance agent, the formidably hip Monsieur Fructus. They would have made a good pair.

Within half an hour, he had made a tour of the minefield on foot, estimated a price, telephoned to order the gravel and given us a firm date, two days away, for his return with the bulldozer. We had our doubts that he was real and, when Menicucci called that evening in his capacity as supervisor of catastrophes, I said that Monsieur Sanchez had surprised us with his efficiency.

'It runs in the family,' Menicucci said. 'His father is a melon millionaire. The son will be a bulldozer millionaire. They are very serious, despite being Spanish.' He explained that Sanchez *père* had come to France as a young man to find work, and had developed a method of producing earlier and more succulent melons than anyone else in Provence. He was now, said Menicucci, so rich that he worked for only two months a year and lived during the winter in Alicante.

Sanchez *fils* arrived as promised, and spent the day re-arranging the landscape with his bulldozer. He had a delicacy of touch that was fascinating to watch, redistributing tons of earth as accurately as if he were using a trowel. When the drive was level, he smoothed the surface with a giant comb, and invited us to see what he had done. It looked too immaculate to walk on, and he had given it a slight camber so that any future downpours would run off into the vines.

'*C'est bon?*'

As good as the autoroute to Paris, we said.

'*Bieng. Je revieng demaing.*' He climbed into the control tower of his bulldozer and drove off at a stately fifteen miles an hour. Tomorrow the gravel would be laid.

The first vehicle to disturb the combed perfection of the drive's surface crawled up to the house the next morning and stopped with a shudder of relief in the parking area. It was a truck that looked to be even more venerable than Faustin's grape wagon, sagging so low on its suspension that the rusty exhaust pipe nearly touched the ground. A man and a woman, both round and weatherbeaten, were standing by the truck and looking with interest at the house, obviously itinerant field workers hoping for one last job before heading further south for the winter.

They seemed a nice old couple, and I felt sorry for them.

'I'm afraid the grapes have all been picked,' I said.

The man grinned and nodded. 'That's good. You were lucky to get them in before the rain.' He pointed up to the forest behind the house. 'Plenty of mushrooms there, I should think.'

Yes, I said, plenty.

They showed no sign of going. I said they were welcome to leave their truck outside the house and pick some mushrooms.

'No, no,' said the man. 'We're working today. My son is on his way with the gravel.'

The melon millionaire opened the back doors of the truck and took out a long-handled mason's shovel and a wide-toothed wooden rake. 'I'll leave the rest for him to unload,' he said. 'I don't want to squash my feet.'

I looked inside. Packed tight up against the back of the seats and stretching the length of the truck was a miniature steam roller, the *compacteur*.

While we waited for his son, Monsieur Sanchez talked about life and the pursuit of happiness. Even after all these years, he said, he still enjoyed the occasional day of manual labour. His work with the melons was finished by July, and he got bored with nothing to do. It was very agreeable to be rich, but one needed something else, and, as he liked working with his hands, why not help his son?

I had never employed a millionaire before. I don't have much time for them as a rule, but this one put in a good long day. Load after load of gravel was delivered and tipped on to the drive by the son. The father shovelled and spread, and Madame Sanchez followed behind with the wooden rake, pushing and smoothing. Then the *compacteur* was unloaded; it was like a massive baby carriage with handlebars, and it was wheeled ceremoniously up and down the drive with Sanchez the son at the controls, shouting instructions at his parents – another shovelful here, more raking there, mind your feet, don't tread on the vines.

It was a true family effort, and by the end of the afternoon we had a pristine ribbon of crushed, putty-coloured gravel worthy of being entered for the Concours d'Elégance sponsored by *Bulldozer Magazine*. The *compacteur* was inserted into the back of the truck; the parents into the front. Young Sanchez said that the price would be less than his estimate, but he would work it out exactly and his father would come round to deliver the bill.

The next morning when I got up, there was an unfamiliar van parked outside the house. I looked for a driver, but there was nobody in the vines or in the outbuildings. It was probably an idle hunter who couldn't be bothered to walk up from the road.

We were finishing breakfast when there was a tap on the window

167

and we saw the round brown face of Monsieur Sanchez. He wouldn't come into the house, because he said his boots were too dirty. He had been in the forest since six o'clock, and he had a present for us. From behind his back he produced his old checked cap, bulging with wild mushrooms. He gave us his favourite recipe – oil, butter, garlic and chopped parsley – and told us a dreadful story about three men who had died after an ill-chosen mushroom supper. A neighbour had found them still at the table with wide, staring eyes – Monsieur Sanchez gave us a demonstration, rolling his eyes back in his head – completely paralysed by malignant fungus. But we were not to worry, he said. He would stake his life on the mushrooms in his cap. *Bon appétit!*

My wife and I ate them that evening, studying each other between mouthfuls for signs of paralysis and eye-rolling. They tasted so much better than ordinary mushrooms that we decided to invest in a guide book and to share a pair of anti-snake boots.

* * * * *

There comes a time in the restoration of an old house when the desire to see it finished threatens all those noble aesthetic intentions to see it finished properly. The temptation to settle for the short cut nags away as the delays add up and the excuses multiply: the carpenter has severed a fingertip, the mason's truck has been stolen, the painter has *la grippe*, fittings ordered in May and promised for June don't arrive until September, and all the time the concrete-mixer and the rubble and the shovels and pickaxes become more and more like permanent fixtures. During the hot months of summer, tranquillised by the sun, it had been possible to look with a patient eye at the uncompleted jobs throughout the house. Now that we were spending more time indoors with them, patience had been replaced by irritation.

With Christian the architect, we went through the rooms to establish who had to do what, and how long it would take.

'*Normalement*,' said Christian, a man of great charm and implacable optimism, 'there is only six or seven days of work. A little masonry, some plastering, two days of painting, *et puis voilà*. *Terminé.*'

We were encouraged. As we said to Christian, there had been dark moments recently when we imagined waking up on Christmas morning still surrounded by the debris of a building site.

He threw up everything in horror – hands, eyebrows and shoulders. What a thought. It was inconceivable that these mere finishing touches should be delayed any longer. He would telephone the various members of the *équipe* immediately to organise a week of intensive activity. Progress would be made. No, more than progress; a conclusion.

One by one, they came at odd times to the house: Didier and his dog at seven in the morning. The electrician at lunchtime, Ramon the plasterer for an evening drink. They came, not to work, but to look at the work that had to be done. They were all astonished that it had taken so long, as though people other than themselves had been responsible. Each of them told us, confidentially, that the problem was always that one had to wait for the other fellow to finish before one could start. But, when we mentioned Christmas, they roared with laughter. Christmas was *months* away; they could almost build a complete house by Christmas. There was, however, a common reluctance to name a day.

When can you come? we asked.

Soon, soon, they said.

We would have to be content with that. We went out to the front of the house, where the concrete-mixer stood guard over the steps to the front door, and imagined a cypress tree standing in its place.

Soon, soon.

NOVEMBER

The French peasant is an inventive man, and he hates waste. He is reluctant to discard anything, because he knows that one day the bald tractor tyre, the chipped scythe, the broken hoe and the gearbox salvaged from the 1949 Renault van will serve him well and save him from disturbing the contents of that deep, dark pocket where he keeps his money.

The contraption that I found at the edge of the vineyard was a rusty monument to his ingenuity. A 100-litre oil drum had been sliced in half lengthways and mounted on a framework of narrow-gauge iron piping. An old wheel, more oval than round, had been bolted on to the front. Two handles of unequal length protruded from the back. It was, so Faustin told me, a *brouette de vigneron* – a wheelbarrow, purpose-built at minimal expense for the pruning season.

All the vines had now been stripped of their leaves by the autumn winds, and the tangled shoots looked like coiled clumps of brown barbed wire. Some time before the sap started to rise next spring they would have to be cut back to the main stem. The clippings, or *sarments*, were of no agricultural use, too fibrous to rot into the ground during the winter, and too numerous to leave piled in the corridors between the vines where the tractors would

170

pass. They would have to be gathered up and burnt; hence the *brouette de vigneron*.

It was the simplest kind of mobile incinerator. A fire was lit in the bottom of the oil drum, the *sarments* were clipped and thrown on the fire, and the barrow was pushed along to the next vine. When the drum was full, the pale grey ash was scattered on the ground and the process began again. It was, in its primitive way, a model of efficiency.

Walking back to the house just before dusk, I saw a slim plume of blue smoke rising from the corner of the field where Faustin was pruning and burning. He straightened up and rubbed his back, and his hand felt cold and stiff when I shook it. He pointed along the rows of clipped vines, twisted claws black against the sandy soil.

'Nice and clean, eh? I like to see them nice and clean.' I asked him to leave some *sarments* for me to gather up to use on the barbecue next summer, and I remembered seeing them once in a shop which called itself a food boutique in New York – Genuine Vine Clippings, they were labelled, and they were guaranteed to impart That Authentic Barbecue Flavor. They had been trimmed to a standard length and neatly trussed with straw twine, and they cost two dollars for a small bunch. Faustin couldn't believe it.

'People buy them?'

He looked at the vines again, estimating how many hundreds of dollars he had burned in the course of the day, and shook his head. Another cruel blow. He shrugged.

'*C'est curieux.*'

* * * * *

Our friend, who lived deep in Côtes du Rhône country north of Vaison-la-Romaine, was to be honoured by the winegrowers of his village and admitted to the Confrérie Saint-Vincent, the local equivalent of the Chevaliers du Tastevin. The investiture was to take place in the village hall, followed by dinner, followed by dancing. The wines would be strong and plentiful and the winegrowers and their wives would be out in force. Ties were to be worn. It was that kind of occasion.

Years before, we had been to another Chevaliers' dinner, in Burgundy. Two hundred people in full evening dress, rigid with decorum at the start of the meal, had turned into a friendly mob singing Burgundian drinking songs by the time the main course was served. We had blurred but happy memories of watching the sozzled Chevaliers after dinner, trying to find and then to unlock their cars, with the amiable assistance of the Clos Vougeot police force. It had been our first experience of an evening formally dedicated to mass intoxication, and we had enjoyed it enormously. Any friend of the grape was a friend of ours.

The village hall was officially called the *Salle des Fêtes*. It was a fairly recent construction, designed with a complete disregard for its mediaeval surroundings by the anonymous and overworked French architect whose mission in life is to give every village its own eyesore. This was a classic of the contemporary blockhouse school – a box of raw brick and aluminium-trimmed glass set in a garden of tarmac, devoid of charm but rich in neon light fittings.

We were greeted at the door by two substantial, rosy-faced men in white shirts, black trousers and wide scarlet sashes. We told them we were guests of the new Confrère.

'*Bieng, bieng. Allez-y.*' Meaty hands patted us on the back and into the big room.

At one end was a raised platform, furnished with a long table and a microphone. Smaller tables, set for dinner, were placed down either side of the room and across the far end, leaving a large space in the middle which was packed with wine-growers and their friends.

The level of conversation was deafening; men and women who are used to talking to each other across a vineyard find it difficult to adjust their volume, and the room echoed and boomed with voices that had been developed to compete with the Mistral. But, if the voices had come straight in from the fields, the clothes were definitely from the Sunday-best *armoire*: dark suits and shirts whose collars looked uncomfortably tight round weatherbeaten necks for the men; vividly coloured and elaborate dresses for the women. One couple, more couture-conscious than the rest, had outfits of startling splendour. The woman shimmered in a dress of grey bugle beads, and small matching grey feathers were sewn to the back of her stockings so that her legs appeared to flutter when she walked. Her husband wore a white jacket trimmed with black piping, a frilled shirt with more black piping and black evening trousers. Either his nerve or his resources had run out at that point, because his shoes were sensible, thick-soled and brown. Nevertheless, we felt sure that they were the couple to watch when the dancing started.

We found our friend and his family. He was glancing round the room, looking puzzled and almost ill-at-ease, and we thought that the solemnity of the occasion had brought on an attack of Confrère's nerves. The problem, however, was altogether more serious.

'I can't see a bar anywhere,' he said. 'Can you?'

There were barrels of wine against one of the walls. There were bottles of wine on the tables. We were in a village which would float on a sea of Côtes du Rhône if all the *caves* were emptied, but there was no bar. And, now that we studied our fellow revellers, we made another worrying discovery. Nobody was holding a glass.

We were prevented from making an indiscreet grab at a bottle on the nearest table by a fanfare on the loudspeaker system, and the Confrères filed in and took up their position behind the table on the dais – a dozen or more figures in cloaks and wide-brimmed hats, some holding parchment scrolls, one with an imposingly fat book. Any moment now, we thought, the *vin d'honneur* would be served to signal the start of the ceremony.

The Mayor embraced the microphone and delivered the opening speech. The senior Confrère gave a speech. His assistant, the keeper of the fat book, gave a speech. One by one the three new Confrères were summoned to the dais and eulogised at length for their love of wine and good fellowship. One by one, they replied with speeches accepting the honours bestowed upon them. I detected a certain huskiness in the voice of our friend which others may have mistaken for emotion. I knew it to be thirst.

As a finale, we were asked to join in the singing of a song written in the Provençal language by Frédéric Mistral.

'*Coupo santo e versanto*,' we sang in praise of the sainted and overflowing goblet, '*A-de-reng beguen en troupo lou vin pur de nostre plant*' – let us all drink together the pure wine of our growth, and about time too. The investiture had taken just over an hour, and not a drop had passed anyone's lips.

There was a noticeable eagerness to be seated, and at last the sainted goblets were filled, emptied and refilled. An air of relief spread throughout the tables, and we were able to relax and consider the menu.

Quail in aspic came first; the heads, which we were told cost two francs each, were detachable and could be used again at a future banquet. Then there was sea bass. These were mere preliminaries, the chef's limbering-up exercises before attacking the sirloin of Charolais beef *en croûte*. But, before that, there was a small and deadly item described as a *Trou Provençal* – a sorbet made with the minimum of water and the maximum of *marc*. Its purpose, so we were told, was to clear the palate; in fact it was sufficiently powerful to anaesthetize not only the palate, but the sinus passages and the front portion of the skull as well. But the chef knew what he was doing. After the initial jolt of frozen alcohol wore off, I could feel a hollowness in the stomach – the *trou* – and I could face the rest of the long meal with some hope of being able to finish it.

The beef made its entrance to the strains of a second fanfare, and was paraded around the tables by the waiters and waitresses before being served. The white wine gave way to the pride of the local wine-growers, a formidably heavy red, and the courses kept coming until, after the serving of soufflés and champagne, it was time to rise up and dance.

The band was of the old school, clearly not interested in performing for people who simply like to hop up and down; they wanted to see *dancing*. There were waltzes and quicksteps and several numbers which might have been gavottes, but for me the highlight of the evening was the tango interlude. I don't think it is given to many of us to witness fifty or sixty couples in the advanced stages of inebriation attempting the swoops and turns and heel-stamping flourishes of the true tango artist, and it was a sight I shall never forget. Elbows were cocked, heads flicked from side to side, desperate and off-balance charges were made with twinkling feet from one end of the room to the other, potential collision and disaster was everywhere. One diminutive man danced blind, his head sunk into the *décolletage* of his taller partner. The couple in bugle beads and frilled shirt, moulded together at the groin with their backs arching outwards, lunged and dipped through the crowd with a dexterity unknown outside the tango palaces of Buenos Aires.

Miraculously, nobody was injured. When we left, some time after one o'clock, the music was still playing and the dancers, stuffed with food and awash with wine, were still dancing. Not for the first time, we marvelled at the Provençal constitution.

We arrived back at the house the following day to find that its appearance had changed; there was an unfamiliar tidiness in front of the steps which led up to the door. The cement-mixer, which had for months been an integral part of the façade of the house, was no longer there.

It was an ominous sign. As much as we disliked having its hulk parked outside, it was at least a guarantee that Didier and his masons would return. Now they had crept in and taken it – *our* cement-mixer – probably to use on a six-month job somewhere the other side of Carpentras. Our hopes of having a finished house by Christmas suddenly seemed like a bad attack of misplaced optimism.

Christian, as usual, was sympathetic and reassuring.

'They had to go to Mazan . . . an emergency job . . . the roof of an old widow's house . . .'

I felt guilty. What were our problems compared to the plight of a poor old widow exposed to the elements?

'Don't worry,' Christian said. 'Two days, maybe three, and then they'll be back to finish off. There's plenty of time before Christmas. It's weeks away.'

Not many weeks away, we thought. My wife suggested kidnapping Didier's cocker spaniel, closer to his heart even than the cement-mixer, and keeping it as a hostage. It was a fine, bold scheme, except that the dog never left Didier's side. Well, if not his dog, maybe his wife. We were prepared to consider almost anything.

The unfinished jobs – temporary windows and chinks in the masonry in particular – were made more apparent by the first sustained Mistral of winter. It blew for three days, bending the cypress tree in the courtyard into a green C, tearing at the tatters of plastic in the melon fields, worrying away at loose tiles and shutters, moaning through the night. It was malevolent and inescapable, a wind to lower the spirits as it threw itself endlessly against the house, trying to get in.

'Good weather for suicide,' Massot said to me one morning as the wind flattened his moustache against his cheeks. '*Beh oui*. If this continues, we'll see a funeral or two.'

Of course, he said, this was nothing like the Mistrals of his boyhood. In those days, the wind blew for weeks on end, doing strange and horrible things to the brain. He told me the story of Arnaud, a friend of his father's.

Arnaud's horse was old and tired and no longer strong enough for farm work. He decided to sell it and buy a fresh young horse, and walked the fifteen kilometres to Apt market one windy morning leading the old nag behind him. A buyer was found, the price was agreed, but the young horses for sale that day were poor, thin specimens. Arnaud walked home alone. He would return next week in the hope that better animals would be on sale.

The Mistral continued all that week, and was still blowing when Arnaud walked again to Apt market. This time he was lucky, and bought a big dark horse. It cost him almost double what he had made on the sale of the old horse, but, as the dealer said, he was paying for youth. The new horse had years of work in him.

Arnaud was only two or three kilometres from his farm when the horse broke free from its leading rein and bolted. Arnaud ran after it until he could run no more. He searched in the scrub and in the vineyards, shouting into the wind, cursing the Mistral that had unsettled the horse, cursing his bad luck, cursing his lost money. When it became too dark to search any longer, he made his way home, angry and despairing. Without a horse, he couldn't work the land; he would be ruined.

His wife met him at the door. An extraordinary thing had happened: a horse, a big dark horse, had come running up the track and had gone into one of the outbuildings. She had given it water and pulled a cart across the opening to block its escape.

Arnaud took a lantern and went to look at the horse. A broken lead rein hung from its head. He touched its neck, and his fingers came away stained. In the light of the lantern, he could see the sweat running down its flanks, and pale patches where the dye had worn off. He had bought back his old horse. In rage and shame he went up into the forest behind his farm and hanged himself.

Massot lit a cigarette, hunching his shoulders and cupping his hands against the wind.

'At the inquest,' he said, 'someone had a sense of humour. The cause of death was recorded as suicide while the balance of the mind was disturbed by a horse.'

Massot grinned and nodded. All his stories, it seemed, ended brutally.

'But he was a fool,' Massot said. 'He should have gone back and shot the dealer who sold him the horse – *paf*! – and blamed it on the Mistral. That's what I'd have done.' His reflections on the nature of justice were interrupted by the whine of an engine in low gear, and a Toyota four-wheel-drive truck, as wide as the footpath, slowed down briefly to give us time to jump out of the way. It was Monsieur Dufour, the village grocer and scourge of the Lubéron's *sanglier* population.

We had seen the heads of *sangliers* mounted on the walls of butchers' shops, and had paid no more attention to them than to any other of the strange rustic decorations that we saw from time to time. But once or twice during the summer the *sangliers* had come down from the dry upper slopes of the mountain to drink from the swimming pool and steal melons, and we could never look a stuffed head in the eye again after seeing the living animals. They were black and stout and longer in the leg than a conventional pig, with worried, whiskery faces. We loved our rare glimpses of them, and wished that the hunters would leave them alone. Unfortunately, *sangliers* taste like venison, and are consequently chased from one end of the Lubéron to the other.

Monsieur Dufour was the acknowledged champion hunter, a modern and mechanised Nimrod. Dressed in his combat uniform, his truck bristling with high-powered armaments, he could drive up the rocky trails and reach the *sanglier*-infested upper slopes while less well-equipped hunters were still coughing their way up on foot. On the flat bed of his truck was a large wooden chest containing six hounds, trained to track for days on end. The poor old pigs didn't stand much of a chance.

I said to Massot that I thought it was a shame the *sangliers* were hunted quite so relentlessly by so many hunters.

'But they taste delicious,' he said. 'Specially the young ones, the *marcassins*. And besides, it's natural. The English are too sentimental about animals, except those men who chase foxes, and they are mad.'

The wind was strengthening and getting colder, and I asked Massot how long he thought it would last.

'A day, a week. Who knows?' He leered at me. 'Not feeling like suicide, are you?'

I said I was sorry to disappoint him, but I was well and cheerful, looking forward to the winter and Christmas.

'Usually a lot of murders after Christmas.' He said it as though he was looking forward to a favourite television programme, a bloody sequel to the Mistral suicides.

I heard gunfire as I walked home, and I hoped Dufour had missed. No matter how long I lived here, I would never make a true countryman. And, as long as I preferred to see a wild boar on the hoof instead of on the plate, I'd never make an adopted Frenchman. Let him worship his stomach; I would maintain a civilised detachment from the bloodlust that surrounded me.

This noble smugness lasted until dinner. Henriette had given us a wild rabbit, which my wife had roasted with herbs and mustard. I had two helpings. The gravy, thickened with blood, was wonderful.

* * * * *

Madame Soliva, the eighty-year-old chef whose *nom de cuisine* was Tante Yvonne, had first told us about an olive oil that she said was the finest in Provence. She had better credentials than anyone we knew. Apart from being a magnificent cook, she was olive oil's answer to a Master of Wine. She had tried them all, from Alziari in Nice to the United Producers of Nyons, and in her expert and considered view the oil produced in the valley of Les Baux was the best. One could buy it, she told us, from the little mill in Maussane-les-Alpilles.

When we lived in England, olive oil had been a luxury, to be saved for the making of fresh mayonnaise and the dressing of salads. In Provence, it was an abundant daily treat which we

bought in five-litre *bidons* and used for cooking, for marinating goats' cheeses and red peppers, and for storing truffles. We dipped our bread in it, bathed our lettuce in it and even used it as a hangover preventative. (One tablespoon of oil, taken neat before drinking, was supposed to coat the stomach and protect it against the effects of too much young pink wine.) We soaked up olive oil like sponges, and gradually learned to distinguish between different grades and flavours. We became fussy and no doubt insufferable about our oil, never buying it from shops or supermarkets, but always from a mill or a producer, and I looked forward to oil-buying expeditions almost as much as trips to the vineyards.

An essential part of a day out is lunch, and before going anywhere new we always studied the Gault-Millau guide as well as the map. We discovered that Maussane was perilously close to the Baumanière at Les Baux, where the bills are as memorable as the cooking, but we were saved from temptation by Madame Soliva. 'Go to Le Paradou,' she told us, 'and have lunch at the café. And make sure you're there by noon.'

It was a cold, bright day, good eating weather, and we walked into the Bistro du Paradou a few minutes before midday with appetites sharpened by the smell of garlic and woodsmoke that greeted us. An enormous fire, a long room filled with old marble-topped tables, a plain tiled bar, a busy clatter coming from the kitchen – it had everything. Except, as the *patron* explained, somewhere for us to sit.

The room was still empty, but he said it would be full within fifteen minutes. He shrugged in apology. He looked at my wife, so near and yet so far from a good lunch, her face a study in tragic deprivation. At the sight of a woman so clearly in distress, he relented, sat us at a table facing the fire, and put a thick glass carafe of red wine between us.

The regulars started coming through the door in noisy groups, going straight to the places they occupied every day. By 12.30 every seat was taken and the *patron*, who was also the only waiter, was a plate-laden blur.

The restaurant worked on the simple formula of removing the burden of decision from its customers. As in the station café at

Bonnieux, you ate and drank what you were given. We had a crisp, oily salad and slices of pink country sausage, an *aioli* of snails and cod and hard-boiled eggs with garlic mayonnaise, creamy cheese from Fontvieille and a home-made tart. It was the kind of meal that the French take for granted and tourists remember for years. For us, being somewhere between the two, it was another happy discovery to add to our list, somewhere to come back to on a cold day with an empty stomach in the certain knowledge that we would leave warm and full.

We arrived at the olive oil mill in Maussane two months early. The new crop of olives wouldn't be gathered until January, and that was the time to buy oil at its most fresh. Luckily, said the manager of the mill, last year's crop had been plentiful and there was still some oil left. If we would like to have a look around, he would pack a dozen litres for us to take away.

The official name of the establishment – Coopérative Oléicole de la Vallée des Baux – was almost too long to fit on the front of the modest building that was tucked away at the side of a small road. Inside, every surface seemed to have been rubbed with a fine coating of oil; floors and walls were slick to the touch, the stairs that led up to the sorting platform were slippery underfoot. A group of men sat at a table sticking the Coopérative's ornate gold labels on to bottles and flasks filled with the greenish-yellow oil – pure and natural, as the notice on the wall said, extracted by a single cold pressing.

We went into the office to pick up the squat, two-litre jugs that the manager had packed in a carton for us, and he presented each of us with bars of olive oil soap.

'There is nothing better for the skin,' he said, and he patted his cheeks with dainty fingertips. 'And, as for the oil, it is a masterpiece. You'll see.'

Before dinner that night, we tested it, dripping it on to slices of bread that had been rubbed with the flesh of tomatoes. It was like eating sunshine.

* * * * *

The guests continued to come, dressed for high summer and hoping for swimming weather, convinced that Provence enjoyed a Mediterranean climate and dismayed to find us in sweaters, lighting fires in the evening, drinking winter wines and eating winter food.

Is it always as cold as this in November? Isn't it hot all the year round? They would look dejected when we told them about snowdrifts and sub-zero nights and bitter winds, as though we had lured them to the North Pole under false tropical pretences.

Provence has been accurately described as a cold country with a high rate of sunshine, and the last days of November were as bright and as blue as May, clean and exhilarating and, as far as Faustin was concerned, profoundly ominous. He was predicting a savage winter, with temperatures so low that olive trees would die of cold as they had done in 1976. He speculated with grim enjoyment about chickens being frozen stiff and old people turning blue in their beds. He said there would undoubtedly be extended power cuts, and warned me to have the chimney swept.

'You'll be burning wood night and day,' he said, 'and that's when chimneys catch fire. And when the *pompiers* come to put out the fire they'll charge you a fortune unless you have a certificate from the chimneysweep.'

And it could be much worse than that. If the house burnt down as the result of a chimney fire, the insurance company wouldn't pay out unless one could produce a certificate. Faustin looked at me, nodding gravely as I absorbed the thoughts of being cold, homeless and bankrupt, and all because of an unswept chimney.

But what would happen, I asked him, if the certificate had been burnt with the house? He hadn't thought of that, and I think he was grateful to me for suggesting another disastrous possibility. A connoisseur of woe needs fresh worries from time to time, or he will become complacent.

I arranged for Cavaillon's premier chimneysweep, Monsieur Beltramo, to come up to the house with his brushes and suction cleaners. A tall man with a courtly manner and an aquiline, sooty profile, he had been a chimney sweep for twenty years. Not once, he told me, had a chimney cleaned by him ever caught fire. When he was finished, he made out the *certificat de ramonage*, complete with smudged fingermarks, and wished me a pleasant winter. 'It won't be a cold one this year,' he said. 'We've had three cold winters in a row. The fourth is always mild.'

I asked him if he was going to clean Faustin's chimney, and exchange weather forecasts.

'No. I never go there. His wife sweeps the chimney.'

DECEMBER

The postman drove at high speed up to the parking area behind the house and reversed with great élan into the garage wall, crushing a set of rear lights. He didn't appear to have noticed the damage as he came into the courtyard, smiling broadly and waving a large envelope. He went straight to the bar, planted his elbow and looked expectant.

'*Bonjour, jeune homme!*'

I hadn't been called young man for years, and it wasn't the postman's normal habit to bring the mail into the house. Slightly puzzled, I offered him the drink that he was waiting for.

He winked. 'A little pastis,' he said. 'Why not?'

Was it his birthday? Was he retiring? Had he won the big prize in the Loterie Nationale? I waited for him to explain the reason for his high spirits, but he was too busy telling me about the *sanglier* that his friend had shot the previous weekend. Did I know how to prepare these creatures for the pot? He took me through the whole gory process, from disembowelment to hanging, quartering and cooking. The pastis disappeared – it wasn't, I realised, his first of the morning – and a refill accepted. Then he got down to business.

'I have brought you the official Post Office calendar,' said the postman. 'It shows all the Saints' Days, and there are some agreeable pictures of young ladies.'

He took the calendar from its envelope and leafed through the pages until he found a photograph of a girl wearing a pair of coconut shells.

'*Voilà!*'

I told him that he was most kind to think of us, and thanked him.

'It's free,' he said. 'Or you can buy it if you want to.'

He winked again, and I finally understood the purpose of the visit. He was collecting his Christmas tip, but since it would be undignified simply to arrive at the front door with an outstretched hand, we had to observe the ritual of the calendar.

He took his money and finished his drink and roared off to his next call, leaving the remnants of his rear light on the drive.

My wife was looking at the calendar when I came back into the house.

'Do you realise,' she said, 'that it's only three weeks until Christmas, and there's still no sign of the builders?'

And then she had an idea that only a woman could have had. It was obvious, she thought, that the birthday of Jesus Christ was not a sufficiently important deadline for the completion of work on the house. Somehow or other, Christmas would come and go and it would be February by the time everyone recovered from their New Year hangovers and holidays. What we should do was to invite the builders to a party to celebrate the end of the job. But not just the builders; their wives must come too.

The intuitive cunning of this suggestion was based on two assumptions. First, that the wives, who never saw the work that their husbands did in other people's houses, would be so curious that they would find the invitation irresistible. And second, that no wife would want her husband to be the one not to have finished his part of the work. This would cause loss of face among the other wives and public embarrassment, followed by some ugly recriminations in the car on the way home.

It was an inspiration. We fixed a date for the last Sunday before Christmas and sent out the invitations: champagne from 11 o'clock onwards.

Within two days, the cement-mixer was back in front of the house. Didier and his assistants, cheerful and noisy, resumed where they had left off as though there had never been a three-month hiatus. No excuses were made, and no direct explanation given for the sudden return to work. The closest Didier came to it was when he mentioned casually that he wanted to have everything finished before he went skiing. He and his wife, he said, would be delighted to accept our invitation.

We had worked out that if everyone came there would be twenty-two people, all with good Provençal appetites. And, as it was so close to Christmas, they would be looking for something a little more festive than a bowlful of olives and a few slices of *saucisson*. My wife started making lists of provisions, and terse footnotes and reminders were scattered throughout the house: Rabbit terrine! *Gambas* and mayonnaise! Individual pizzas! Mushroom tart! Olive bread! How many quiches? – the scraps of paper were everywhere, making my one-word list – champagne – look sparse and inadequate.

The gastronomic highlight was delivered one cold morning by a friend who had relatives in Périgord. It was an entire foie gras – raw, and therefore a fraction of the price of the prepared product. All we had to do was cook it and add some slivers of black truffle.

We unwrapped it. The previous owner must have been a bird the size of a small aircraft, because the liver was enormous – a rich, dark yellow mass that filled both my hands when I lifted it on to the chopping board. Following our friend's instructions, I cut it up and compressed it into glass preserving jars, inserting pieces of truffle with nervous fingers. This was like cooking money.

The jars were sealed, and placed in a huge saucepan of boiling water for precisely ninety minutes. After cooling off, they were refrigerated, then laid to rest in the *cave*. My wife crossed foie gras off her list.

It felt strange to be coming to the end of the year under blue skies, and without the frenzy that characterises the weeks before an English Christmas. The only hint of festive preparations in our valley was the strange noise coming from the house of Monsieur Poncet, about a mile away from us. On two successive mornings as I walked past, I heard terrible squawks – not cries of fear or pain, but of outrage. I didn't think they were human, but I wasn't sure. I asked Faustin if he had noticed them.

'Oh, that,' he said. 'Poncet is grooming his ass.'

On Christmas Eve, there was to be a living *crèche* in the church in Ménerbes, and the ass of Monsieur Poncet had an important supporting role. Naturally, he had to look his best, but he had an aversion to being brushed and combed, and he was not the kind of ass to suffer grooming quietly. Doubtless he would be presentable on the night, said Faustin, but one would be wise to stay well away from his hind legs, as he was reputed to have an impressive kick.

Up in the village, casting was in progress for the Infant Jesus. Babies of a suitable age and disposition were required to present themselves, and temperament – the ability to rise to the big occasion – would be all-important, as the proceedings did not start until midnight.

Apart from that, and the cards that the postman stuffed in the mailbox, Christmas might have been months away. We did not have a television, and so we were spared the sight of those stupefyingly jolly commercials. There were no carol singers, no office parties, no strident countdowns of the remaining shopping days. I loved it. My wife was not so sure; something was missing. Where was my Christmas spirit? Where was the mistletoe? Where was the Christmas tree? We decided to go into Cavaillon to find them.

We were rewarded at once by the sight of Santa Claus. Dressed in baggy red *bouclé* trousers, a Rolling Stones T-shirt, red fur-trimmed pixie hat and false beard, he came weaving towards us as we walked down the Cours Gambetta. It looked from a distance as though his beard was on fire, but as he came closer we saw the stub of a Gauloise among the whiskers. He lurched past in a cloud of Calvados fumes, attracting considerable attention from a group of small children. Their mothers would have some explaining to do.

The streets were strung with lights. Music came through the

open doorways of bars and shops. Christmas trees were stacked in clumps on the pavement. A man with a throat microphone was selling bedlinen from a stall in an alley. 'Take a look at that, Madame. Pure Dralon! I'll give you five thousand francs if you can find a fault in it!' An old peasant woman began a millimetre by millimetre inspection, and the man snatched it away.

We turned the corner and nearly collided with the carcass of a deer, hanging outside the door of a butcher's shop, gazing blindly at the carcass of a *sanglier* hanging next to it. In the window, a line of tiny nude birds, their necks broken and their heads neatly arranged on their breastbones, were offered as a special pre-Christmas promotion, seven for the price of six. The butcher had closed their beaks and set them in a garnish of evergreen leaves and red ribbon. We shuddered, and moved on.

There was no doubt about the most important ingredient in a Provençal Christmas. Judging by the window displays, the queues and the money changing hands, clothes and toys and stereo equipment and baubles were of incidental importance; the main event of Christmas was food. Oysters and crayfish and pheasant and hare, pâtés and cheeses, hams and capons, gâteaux and pink champagne – after a morning spent looking at it all we were suffering from visual indigestion. With our tree and our mistletoe and our dose of Christmas spirit, we came home.

Two uniformed men were waiting for us, parked outside the house in an unmarked car. The sight of them made me feel guilty, of what, I didn't know, but uniformed men have that effect on me. I tried to think what crimes I had committed recently against the Fifth Republic, and then the two men got out of the car and saluted. I relaxed. Even in France, where bureaucratic formality approaches the level of art, they don't salute before they arrest you.

In fact, they weren't policemen, but firemen, *pompiers* from Cavaillon. They asked if they could come into the house, and I wondered where we had put our chimneysweep's certificate. This was obviously a spot check designed to catch any householder with a soiled flue.

We sat round the dining room table. One of the men opened an attaché case. 'We have brought the official calendar of the Pompiers de Vaucluse.' He laid it on the table.

'As you will see, it shows all the Saints' Days.'

And so it did, just like our Post Office calendar. But, instead of photographs of girls wearing coconut shell brassières, this calendar was illustrated with pictures of firemen scaling tall buildings, administering first aid to accident victims, rescuing mountaineers in distress and manning loaded firehoses. The *pompiers* in rural France provide an overall emergency service, and they will retrieve your dog from a pothole in the mountains or take you to hospital, as well as fight your fires. They are in every way an admirable and deserving body of men.

I asked if a contribution would be acceptable.

'*Bien sûr.*'

We were given a receipt which also entitled us to call ourselves Friends of the Cavaillon Fire Department. After more salutes, the two *pompiers* left to try their luck further up the valley, and we hoped that their training had prepared them for attacks by vicious dogs. Getting a contribution out of Massot would be only marginally less hazardous than putting out a fire. I could imagine him, squinting out from behind his curtains, shotgun at the ready, watching his Alsatians hurl themselves at the intruders. I had once seen the dogs attack the front wheel of a car for want of anything human, ripping away at the tyre as though it were a hunk of raw beef, slavering and spitting out shreds of rubber while the terrified driver endeavoured to reverse out of range, and Massot looked on, smoking and smiling.

We were now a two-calendar family, and as the days before Christmas slipped by we anticipated the delivery of a third, which would be worth a substantial contribution. Every Tuesday, sacks Thursday and Saturday for the past twelve months, the heroes of the sanitation department had stopped at the end of our drive to pick up shamefully large piles of empty bottles, the evil-smelling remains of *bouillabaisse* suppers, dog-food cans broken glasses, sacks of rubble, chicken bones and domestic fall-out of every size and description. Nothing defeated them. No heap, however huge and ripe, was too much for the man who clung to the back of the truck, dropping off at each stop to toss the garbage into an open, greasy hold. In the summer, he must have come close to asphyxiation and, in the winter, close to tears with the cold.

He and his partner eventually turned up in a Peugeot which looked as if it was enjoying its final outing before going to the scrapyard – two cheerful, scruffy men with hard handshakes and pastis breath. On the back seat, I could see a brace of rabbits and some bottles of champagne, and I said that it was good to see them picking up some full bottles for a change.

'It's not the empty bottles we mind,' said one of them. 'But you should see what some people leave for us.' He wrinkled his face and held his nose, little finger extended elegantly in the air. '*Dégeulasse.*'

They were pleased with their tip. We hoped they would go out and have a glorious, messy meal, and let someone else clear up.

* * * * *

Didier was squatting on his haunches with a dustpan and brush, sweeping crumbs of cement out of a corner. It was heartening to see this human machine of destruction engaged in such delicate chores; it meant that his work was over.

He stood up and emptied the dustpan into a paper sack and lit a cigarette. 'That's it,' he said. '*Normalement*, the painter will come tomorrow.' We walked outside, where Eric was loading the shovels and buckets and toolboxes on to the back of the truck. Didier grinned. 'It doesn't bother you if we take the cement-mixer?'

I said I thought we could manage without it, and the two of them pushed it up a plank ramp and roped it tight against the back of the driver's cabin. Didier's spaniel watched the progress of the cement-mixer with her head cocked, and then jumped into the truck and lay along the dashboard.

'*Allez!*' Didier held out his hand. It felt like cracked leather. 'See you on Sunday.'

The painter came the next day, and painted, and left. Jean-Pierre the carpet-layer arrived. The wives had obviously decided that everything should be ready for their state visit.

By Friday night, the carpet was laid except for the last couple of metres.

'I'll come in tomorrow morning,' said Jean-Pierre, 'and you'll be able to move the furniture in the afternoon.'

By midday, all that remained to do was to fit the carpet under a wooden batten at the threshold of the room. It was while Jean-Pierre was drilling the holes to screw in the batten that he went through the hot water pipe which ran under the floor, and a jet of water rose in a small and picturesque fountain, framed by the doorway.

We cut off the water supply, rolled back the sodden carpet, and called Monsieur Menicucci. After a year of alarms and emergencies, I knew his number off by heart, and I knew what his first words would be.

'*Oh là là.*' He meditated in silence for a moment. 'The floor will have to be broken so that I can solder the pipe. You had better warn Madame. There will be a little dust.'

Madame was out buying food. She was expecting to return to a bedroom, bathroom and dressing room that were dry, clean and carpeted. She would be surprised. I advised Jean-Pierre to go home for medical reasons. She would probably want to kill him.

'What's that noise?' she said when I met her as she was parking the car.

'It's Menicucci's jackhammer.'

'Ah yes. Of course.' She was unnaturally, dangerously calm. I was glad Jean-Pierre had left.

Menicucci, in his search for the leak, had drilled out a trench in the floor, and we were able to see the hot water pipe with its neat hole.

'*Bon,*' he said. 'Now we must make sure there's no blockage in the pipe before I solder. You stay there and watch. I will blow through the tap in the bathroom.'

I watched. Menicucci blew. I received a gout of dusty water in the face.

'What do you see?' he shouted from the bathroom.

'Water,' I said.

'*Formidable.* The pipe must be clear.'

He made his repairs, and went home to watch the rugby on television.

We started mopping up, telling each other that it really wasn't too bad. The carpet would dry out. There was barely enough rubble to fill a bucket. The scorch marks from the blowlamp could be painted over. All in all, a long as one disregarded the jagged, gaping trench, it was possible to look at the rooms and consider them finished. In any case, we had no choice. Sunday was only hours away.

We weren't expecting anyone before 11.30, but we had underestimated the magnetic appeal that champagne has for the French, and the first knock on the door came shortly after half past ten. Within an hour, everyone except Didier and his wife had arrived. They lined the walls of the living room, awkward with politeness and dressed in their best, darting away from the sanctuary of the walls from time to time to swoop on the food.

As the waiter in charge of keeping glasses filled, I became aware of yet another fundamental difference between the French and the English. When the English come for drinks, the glass is screwed firmly into the hand while talking, smoking or eating. It is set aside with reluctance to deal with calls of nature that require both hands – blowing the nose or visiting the lavatory – but it is never far away or out of sight.

It is different with the French. They are no sooner given a glass before they put it down, presumably because they find conversation difficult with only one hand free. So the glasses gather in groups, and after five minutes identification becomes impossible. The guests, unwilling to take another person's glass but unable to pick out their own, look with longing at the champagne bottle. Fresh glasses are distributed, and the process repeats itself.

I was wondering how long it would be before our supply of glasses ran out and we had to resort to tea cups when there was the familiar sound of a diesel engine in labour, and Didier's truck pulled up behind the house, and he and his wife came in through the back door. It was strange. I knew that Didier had a car, and his wife was dressed from head to toe in fine brown suède which must have sat very uneasily on the gritty seat of the truck.

Christian came across the room and took me aside.

'I think we might have a little problem,' he said. 'You'd better come outside.'

I followed him. Didier took my wife's arm and followed me. As we walked round the house, I looked back and saw that everyone was coming.

'*Voilà!*' said Christian, and pointed at Didier's truck.

On the back, in the space usually reserved for the cement-mixer, was a bulbous shape, three feet high and four feet across. It was wrapped in brilliant green crêpe paper, and dotted with bows of white and red and blue.

'It's for you from all of us,' said Christian. '*Allez.* Unwrap it.'

Didier made a stirrup with his hands, and with effortless gallantry, his cigarette between his teeth, plucked my wife from the ground and lifted her to shoulder height so that she could step on to the back of the truck. I climbed up after her, and we peeled off the green wrapping.

The last strips of paper came away to applause and some piercing whistles from Ramon the plasterer, and we stood in the sunshine on the back of the truck, looking at the upturned faces that surrounded us, and our present.

It was an antique jardinière, a massive circular tub that had been cut by hand from a single block of stone long before the days of cutting machines. It was thick-sided, slightly irregular, a pale, weathered grey. It had been filled with earth and planted with primulas.

We didn't know what to say or how to say it. Surprised, touched and floundering in our inadequate French, we did the best we could. Mercifully, Ramon cut us short.

'*Merde!* I'm thirsty. That's enough speeches. Let's have a drink.'

The formality of the first hour disappeared. Jackets came off and the champagne was attacked in earnest. The men took their wives round the house, showing off their work, pointing out the English bathroom taps marked 'hot' and 'cold', trying the drawers to check that the carpenter had finished the interiors smoothly, touching everything in the manner of curious children.

Christian organised a team to unload the great stone tub from the truck, and eight tipsy men in their Sunday clothes somehow managed to avoid being maimed as the lethal mass was manoeuvred down two sagging planks and on to the ground. Madame Ramon supervised. '*Ah, les braves hommes,*' she said. 'Mind you don't get your fingernails dirty.'

The Menicuccis were the first to leave. Having acquitted themselves with honour among the pâtes and cheeses and flans and champagne, they were off to a late lunch, but not before observing the niceties. They made a ceremonial tour of the other guests, shaking hands, kissing cheeks, exchanging *bons appétits*. Their farewell lasted fifteen minutes.

The others looked as though they were settled for the remainder of the day, eating and drinking their way steadily through everything within reach. Ramon appointed himself the official comedian, and told a series of jokes which became progressively coarser and funnier. He stopped for a drink after explaining how to determine the sex of pigeons by putting them in the refrigerator.

'What made a nice woman like your wife ever marry a terrible old *mec* like you?' asked Didier.

With great deliberation, Ramon put down his champagne and held his hands out in front of him like a fisherman describing the one that got away. Fortunately, he was prevented from going into further revelations by a large piece of pizza which his wife delivered firmly into his mouth. She had heard the routine before.

As the sun moved across the courtyard and left it in afternoon shadow, the guests began to make their tours of departure, with more hand-shaking and kissing and pauses for one final glass.

'Come and have lunch,' said Ramon. 'Or dinner. What's the time?'

It was three o'clock. After four hours of eating and drinking, we were in no state for the *cous-cous* that Ramon was promoting.

'Ah well,' he said, 'if you're on a diet, *tant pis.*'

He gave his wife the car keys and leaned back in the passenger seat, hands clasped across his stomach, beaming at the thought of a solid meal. He had persuaded the other couples to join him. We waved them off and went back to the empty house, the empty plates and the empty glasses. It had been a good party.

We looked through the window at the old stone tub, bright with flowers. It would take at least four men to move it away from the garage and into the garden, and organising four men in Provence was, as we knew, not something that could be arranged overnight. There would be visits of inspection, drinks, heated arguments. Dates would be fixed, and then forgotten. Shoulders would be shrugged and time would pass by. Perhaps by next spring we would see the tub in its proper place. We were learning to think in seasons instead of days or weeks. Provence wasn't going to change its tempo for us.

Meanwhile, there was enough foie gras left over to have in warm, thin slices with salad, and one surviving bottle of champagne cooling in the shallow end of the swimming pool. We put some more logs on the fire and thought about the imminent prospect of our first Provençal Christmas.

It was ironic. Having had guests throughout the year, who often had to endure great inconvenience and primitive conditions because of the building work, we now had the house, clean and finished, to ourselves. The last guests had left the previous week, and the next were arriving to help us see in the New Year. But on Christmas Day we would be alone.

We woke up to sunshine and a quiet, empty valley, and a kitchen with no electricity. The gigot of lamb that was ready to go into the oven had a reprieve, and we faced the terrible possibility of bread and cheese for Christmas lunch. All the local restaurants would have been booked up for weeks.

It is at time like this, when crisis threatens the stomach, that the French display the most sympathetic side of their nature. Tell them stories of physical injury or financial ruin and they will either laugh or commiserate politely. But tell them you are facing gastronomic hardship, and they will move heaven and earth and even restaurant tables to help you.

We telephoned Maurice, the chef at the Auberge de la Loube in Buoux, and asked him if there had been any cancellations. No. Every seat was taken. We explained the problem. There was a horrified silence, and then: 'You may have to eat in the kitchen, but come anyway. Something will be arranged.'

He sat us at a tiny table between the kitchen door and the open fire, next to a large and festive family.

'I have gigot if you like it,' he said. We told him we had thought of bringing our own and asking him to cook it, and he smiled. 'It's not the day to be without an oven.'

We ate long and well and talked about the months that had gone as quickly as weeks. There was so much we hadn't seen and done:

our French was still an ungainly mixture of bad grammar and builders' slang; we had managed somehow to miss the entire Avignon festival, the donkey races at Goult, the accordion competition, Faustin's family outing to the Basses-Alpes in August, the wine festival in Gigondas, the Ménerbes dog show and a good deal of what had been going on in the outside world. It had been a self-absorbed year, confined mostly to the house and the valley, fascinating to us in its daily detail, sometimes frustrating, often uncomfortable, but never dull or disappointing. And, above all, we felt at home.

Maurice brought glasses of *marc* and pulled up a chair.

"Appy Christmas,' he said, and then his English deserted him. '*Bonne Année.*'

* * * * *

Arthur Eperon
Eperon's French Regional Guides

Arthur Eperon offers you his own recommendations for discovering the charms of these popular regions in France. Enjoy the best of each region: its sumptuous food, fascinating historical sites and essential places to visit, described here with more than a *soupçon* of anecdotes and hints to inspire the seasoned as well as the first-time traveller.

France has been Eperon territory for over forty years. Sharing his experiences of the most varied and beautiful country in Europe, *Eperon's French Regional Guides* are at once authoritative *and* uniquely personal, covering all the popular, and some of the lesser-known, regions of France.

Lot and Quercy £5.99

Calme, tranquilité et repos – that's what this hidden gem of France promises its visitors. A region steeped in history and natural wonders, from the caves at Padirac to the remains of the *bastides* (fortified villages of medieval times) in Lot you'll also find good regional cooking, strong red Cahors wine and air so pure that it, too, seems intoxicating.

Brittany £5.99

Brittany's language, culture and history set it apart from the rest of France. Jutting out into the sea like the prow of a ship, it is a wild and dramatic region, but a particularly welcoming one to the British. Mysterious menhirs at Carnac, the 12th century monastery of St Malo and charming Quimper pottery are all part of the Brittany experience, as are *galettes* – buckwheat pancakes, delicious washed down with Breton cider.

Normandy £5.99

Land of lush rolling hills, dotted with cows, Normandy is world-famous as the home of fiery calvados, fresh Camembert and cool cider. The variety of scenery is captivating – stark chalk cliffs, seaside resorts, old fishing villages, woods and forests and *bocages* (little fields criss-crossed with hedges) – all are found here in Normandy.

Arthur Eperon
Eperon's French Wine Tour £6.95

EXPLORE THE VINEYARDS OF FRANCE THE EPERON WAY

France in a wine drinker's paradise. From the noble vintages of Bordeaux and Burgundy and the exquisite pleasures of Champagne, to the unexpected delights of *vin de pays*, the wines of France remain the most sought after and the yardstick by which all others are measured.

Now, with all his customary authority and enthusiasm, Arthur Eperon takes you on a connoisseur's tour of French vineyards. The book is divided into sixteen areas. Each section contains a map showing the notable wine villages, an introduction which includes the address of the local wine committee or information bureau, advice on what to eat and where to stay, a suggested route for visitors to follow, a detailed description of the wines of the region, and, most importantly, precise information on where you can taste and buy them.

Arthur Eperon's personal recommendations for places to explore and new wines to discover, taste and buy – either en route to a holiday destination or as a complete holiday in itself – reflect his great love for France and his unrivalled, intimate knowledge of her wines, the result of innumerable visits over the last forty years.

This indispensable book will add a completely new dimension to your appreciation, knowledge and enjoyment of the wines of France – even if you read it without leaving home!

A Pan Original

Travellers' France, Le Weekend, The French Selection and *The British Selection* by Arthur Eperon are also available in Pan.

All Pan Books are available at your local bookshop or newsagent, or can be ordered direct from the publisher. Indicate the number of copies required and fill in the form below.

Send to: Pan C. S. Dept
                  Macmillan Distribution Ltd
                  Houndmills Basingstoke RG21 2XS
or phone: 0256 29242, quoting title, author and Credit Card number.

Please enclose a remittance* to the value of the cover price plus £1.00 for the first book plus 50p per copy for each additional book ordered.

*Payment may be made in sterling by UK personal cheque, postal order, sterling draft or international money order, made payable to Pan Books Ltd.

Alternatively by Barclaycard/Access/Amex/Diners

Card No.

Expiry Date

Signature

Applicable only in the UK and BFPO addresses.

While every effort is made to keep prices low, it is sometimes necessary to increase prices at short notice. Pan Books reserve the right to show on covers and charge new retail prices which may differ from those advertised in the text or elsewhere.

NAME AND ADDRESS IN BLOCK LETTERS PLEASE

Name

Address

3/87